Keto Meal Prep

The Complete Ketogenic Meal Prep Cookbook for Beginners | Save Time and Eat Healthier with Keto Meal Prep Recipes

Disclaimer

Life should be easy, right? Making the best food choices for your waistline and your health shouldn't demand that you spend hours in the kitchen. It should be fun. It should be easy. And most of all, it should leave you with plenty of time to get on with doing the stuff you really want to do. The fun stuff.

If you're nodding your head at this bit, know that it's YOU I've created this Keto Meal Prep book for.

Yes, YOU!

You can stick to your Keto eating philosophy, keep your nutrition levels high and still enjoy time to enjoy your life when you follow the tips and enjoy the recipes in this book. Did I mention that the recipes are mouth-wateringly good too?

Having said that, I'm not a medical professional. I'm not a chef and I'm certainly not a doctor. So please consult a medical professional before you make changes to your diet or lifestyle.

By eating the delicious food in this cookbook, you do so at your own risk and assume all associated risk involved. Not that there's anything to worry about, but it's worth mentioning anyway.

No responsibility is taken for any loss or damage related directly or indirectly to the information in this book. Never disregard professional medical advice or delay in seeking it because of something you have read in this book or in any linked materials.

Table of Contents

Introduction 7

What to expect in this book...8

Chapter 1: What is the Ketogenic Diet? **9**

How does Keto work?...9

Isn't that just the same as Atkins? 10

What will I be eating? 10

Are there any side effects from this diet?...............................10

Is Keto safe for everyone? 10

Who invented Keto? 11

What are the benefits of the Keto diet?..................................11

Chapter 2: Keto eating: What's ON the Menu and What's NOT **13**

Here's what's ON the menu.. 13

Here's what's OFF the menu 17

Chapter 3: What is Meal Prepping? **20**

Why meal prep foods for the Keto diet? 21

How to Meal Prep 21

Chapter 4: Ketogenic Meal Prep Recipes **25**

Breakfast...25

Sausage and Egg Breakfast Sandwich 25

Avocado Egg Breakfast 26

Breakfast Pumpkin Bread...27

Stuffed Breakfast Biscuits...29

Italian Breakfast Casserole 30

Overnight Chia Oatmeal 31

Blueberry Bread..32

Greek Egg Bake..34

Turmeric Scrambled Eggs 35

Cauliflower Hash Browns 36

Blueberry Pancake Bites 37

Sausage Ball Puffs 38

Acai Almond Butter Smoothie 39

Cauliflower and Ground Beef Omelet 40

Ultimate Keto Bagels 42

Blackberry Egg Bake 43

Cauliflower Fritters 44

Lunch 45

White Turkey Chili 45

Curry Chicken Lettuce Wraps 46

Cheddar-Wrapped Taco Rolls 47

Fully-Loaded Chicken Salad 48

Sesame Salmon with Baby Bok Choy & Mushrooms 50

Almond Butter Bacon Burger 51

Shrimp Avocado Salad with Tomatoes and Feta...................53

Thai Chicken Noodle Soup 54

Lasagna Stuffed Portobellos 55

Marinated Cauliflower Antipasto Salad 56

Italian Chicken Bowls 57

Thai Tuna Salad 59

Broccoli & Cheese Soup 60

Caribbean Jerk Shrimp with Cauliflower Rice.......................62

Asian Chicken and Rainbow Veggies 64

Mushroom and Feta Casserole 65

Caesar Salad..66

Thai Coconut Soup with Shrimp or Chicken..........................67

Lime Chicken Chowder...68

Pork Egg Roll in a Bowl 69

Vietnamese Banh Mi Meatballs...70

Keto Bacon Sausage Meatballs 72

Cream Cheese & Salami Pinwheels 73

Cheeseburger Lettuce Wraps 74

Chicken Enchilada Bowl 75

Flaxseed Keto Wraps 76

Italian Sub Roll-Ups 77

Chicken Tenders 78

Avocado Egg Salad (No Mayo) 79

Keto Poke with Ahi Tuna and Citrus 80

Bacon, Chicken & Tomato Stuffed Avocado 81

Avocado Tuna Salad 82

Dinners 83

The Ultimate Low-Carb Stir-Fry 83

Cauliflower Fried Rice 84

Spiralized Pad Thai Chicken 85

Greek Chicken Meal Prep Bowls 86

Mediterranean Broccoli Salad 87

Zucchini Enchiladas 88

Sesame Chicken 90

Bacon Ranch Chicken Casserole 91

Sheet Pan Chicken Fajitas 92

Loaded Cauliflower Bake 93

Turkey Sausage Frittata 94

Berbere Stuffed Peppers 95

Creamy Mushroom Chicken 96

Shrimp Stir Fry with Cauliflower Rice 97

Spicy Mustard Thyme Chicken & Coconut Roasted Brussels Sprouts 98

Keto Pizza Crust 99

Lemon Chicken with Asparagus 100

Cheesesteak Stuffed Bell Peppers 101

Keto Lasagna with Zucchini Noodles 102

Buffalo Wings 103

Snacks & Sides 104

Cheesy Bacon Stuffed Mini Peppers 104

Superfood Meatballs 105

Steak Bites 107

Lemon Cashew Cookies 108

Peaches and Cream Fat Bombs 109

Avocado Brownies 110

Taco Cups 111

Cheesy Cloud Biscuits 112

Chocolate & Peanut Butter Keto Bites 113

Keto Marinara Sauce 114

Worcestershire Sauce 115

Final words **116**

Introduction

Sitting down to write the introduction of a book like this, it's *insanely* hard to know where to start.

Do I start by telling you about the wonders of the Ketogenic diet and how it's helped me to drop an astonishing amount of weight that would never seem to shift, despite me trying practically every slimming diet out there?

Should I be telling you that this amazing diet has boosted my energy levels like nothing before, increased my stamina, lifted my productivity levels and healed a ton of niggling health complaints that I never seemed to be able to shift?

No. Maybe you'd prefer to hear about the magic of meal prep.

Maybe you'd love me to tell you that meal has transformed my relationship with food even more than the Keto diet ever did.

That it has saved me more time and money than I'd ever dreamed possible.

That instead of slaving away in the kitchen for hours every day, I could get it all done in an hour or two per week, then sit back and relax whilst enjoying the delicious food I'd created.

Because all of this is true.

This is exactly what I've experienced since I combined my passions for the Keto diet and my obsession for organization.

One minute, I was just a regular adult (apart from my secret love of ABBA and retro videogames!). I spent my life eating too much junk food, feeling fat and unattractive, getting progressively sicker and feeling tired the whole day long. I didn't have energy for anything other than climbing into my car, heading to work and coming right back again. Life sucked, if I'm completely honest with you!

Then I discover the Keto diet, and everything changed.

The weight fell off, the brain fog lifted, and it felt as if a brand new me stepped out into the world. It was amazing!

Despite my enthusiasm, spending all that time in the kitchen did lose its appeal after a while. I'd been used to takeaways and cheap all-you-can-eat dinners.

What the hell was I doing in a kitchen for hours on end?

I was ready to quit. Regardless of those life-changing benefits of Keto, I was sick of spending my time like this.

But then my friend introduced me to the wonderful world of meal prep, and I was converted! I was hooked! And I've never looked back since.

You see, you CAN 'have your cake and eat it'. You can eat healthily and enjoy your food, without spending your life in the kitchen. Let me tell you how.

What to expect in this book

This isn't a massive book, and we have a ton of information to cover here so let me give you a quick overview.

We'll start by looking at the Ketogenic diet itself, covering the basics, the health benefits, the important facts you need to know and finally, covering the foods that you can and can't eat on the Keto diet.

Then we'll turn our attention to meal prep and I'll walk you through everything you need to know, including the precise steps you need to take to make meal prep part of your life, the tricks I use every day to get even better organized, and any other information I think you should know.

Finally, we come to the best part of all- the recipes!

I'll be sharing tons of easy-to-make, mouth-watering Keto recipes with you that you can make part of your meal prep life right away.

These are split into breakfast, lunch, dinner, and snack and sides for ease of reference. However, don't feel like you have to stick to eating these foods at these times.

If you want to eat blueberry pancakes for dinner, then please go ahead.

I've also done the best I can to keep it simple for you. Whilst you might find the occasional slightly unusual ingredient in the recipes, I've done my best to offer alternatives wherever possible.

And finally, whilst I personally follow the Keto diet relatively strictly, I understand that not everyone operates under this philosophy.

That's why I've made the effort to some recipes which use slightly higher carb ingredients. But don't feel like you need to include them! Substitute ingredients to your hearts content and really make your meals something to remember.

Now I've got you here and I have your attention, why not join me as I lead you through the wonderful world of Keto meal prep. Let's go!

Chapter 1: What is the Ketogenic Diet?

The Ketogenic diet is a revolution in eating.

It's a revolution in health.

And it's about to revolutionize your waistline, your energy levels, your sleep patterns and leave you feeling like a brand new you.

Want to know what the best bit of all is?

It's the fact you can eat all the delicious, satisfying foods that you love (yes, even the creamy rich ones!) and still watch the weight fall off. It feels like a miracle when you've seen it happening with your own eyes. But it's 100% real.

You can wave goodbye to those horrible fad diets which leave you feeling deprived, drain your bank account and leave you fighting hunger pangs. You won't have to force down food that you hate or nibble salad like a rabbit.

It's all about **eating the food you love, as much of it as you want and still losing weight.**

I know it sounds too good to be true.

Especially if you've been brought up with the old wisdom about food, exercise and weight loss.

Because you don't need to sweat in the gym for hours on end to shift that stubborn weight. You don't need to starve yourself.

You just need to discover the Keto diet.

How does Keto work?

The magic happens on the Keto diet because you're switching from using carbs and sugars as your fuel source, to protein and fat. Yes, it's that simple.

As we all know, carbs and sugars are largely empty calories which cause you to gain weight and store it in all the worst places. I'm talking hips, stomach, butt and arms.

When you shift to fueling your body with fats and proteins, it will burn the fat right away from those trouble spots in your body, so you can literally go to bed one night and wake up several pounds lights. Awesome, huh?

Isn't that just the same as Atkins?

Well spotted! There are *huge* similarities between the Ketogenic diet and the Atkins diet, but the diets are certainly NOT the same thing.

On the Keto diet you're barely eating any carbs at all and aiming to reach a state of Ketosis where your body switches to using fat and protein instead of carbs. This isn't the case with Atkins. The Keto diet places a huge emphasis on the consumption of healthy fats, whereas Atkins is all about the protein.

Keto will help the weight effortlessly fall off, Atkins will just encourage it to shift.

Both are good. But Keto is better.

What will I be eating?

Keep reading to find out the exact foods you can enjoy on this wonderful diet- I've gone into more detail in the chapter that comes.

Overall, your food intake will break down to about 70-80% fat, 25% protein and up to 5% carbs.

Are there any side effects from this diet?

As with any lifestyle change, you can expect a few minor symptoms when you switch to Keto.

This is usually caused by your body switching over to using fats as its main fuel, and it's nothing to worry about. It's often referred to as 'Keto flu' as it's so common. It doesn't last for long and is best treated with chilling out, drinking plenty of water and sleeping whenever you can, so don't worry.

Bear in mind that you don't need to enter this state (called 'ketosis') to lose weight on the Keto diet- you can still eat some carbs and enjoy some of the amazing health benefits of this diet.

Is Keto safe for everyone?

Yes, the Ketogenic diet is safe for everyone, both young and old. Even children can use the Ketogenic diet (but only under doctor's supervision). Having said that, it's always worth seeking medical advice if you are suffering with a chronic health condition, you're suffering with diabetes, you have high blood pressure or you're pregnant or breastfeeding.

Who invented Keto?

Originally, the Keto diet was introduced as a way of controlling certain types of epilepsy in children.

However, many people started to notice how beneficial it was for weight loss and health, so more and more people started to experiment with this break-through way of eating.

And boy, have the results been astonishing! Now it's one of the most all-time popular diets and continues to transform the health of millions of people across the globe.

What are the benefits of the Keto diet?

Most people want to hear that the Keto diet will help them shift that weight they've been carrying for so long. But there are actually many varied health benefits which you could start enjoying today if you switch to Keto. These include:

Benefit #1: Weight loss. You'll shift weight without really trying, even whilst you sleep.

Benefit #2: Brain boost. Your thinking powers will get a well-deserved boost with the Keto diet. It's because of those healthy fats.

Benefit #3: Increased stamina. It's much easier to fuel yourself with fat than carbs. Just look at any car engine for evidence. This means you'll be able to further for longer.

Benefit #4: Balanced hormones. Carbs spell disaster for hormone balance and health. Cut them out and you'll heal your hormonal issues and feel awesome again.

Benefit #5: Less hunger. You won't feel hungry on Keto. Trust me!

Benefit #6: A healthier heart. Reduced carbs mean less bad cholesterol flowing around your body and a reduced risk of heart disease.

Benefit #7: Less migraines. There's a growing body of research which shows that the Keto diet reduces levels of glutamate in the brain, and therefore reduces migraine attacks.

Benefit #8: Protection against cancer. Cancerous cells in your body fed off sugars and carbs. Reduce your intake of these foods and you cut off their supply.

Benefit #9: Fewer symptoms of epilepsy. As you've already read, the Keto diet was invented for you, so don't be surprised when your symptoms improve.

So, whether you want to shift that weight, protect your health, get more energy, health your lingering health problems, and give your productivity a boost, the Keto diet is undoubtedly the right solution for you.

Now you just need to get started!

But before we do, I want to take some time to run through what you can eat on the Keto diet, and what you need to start avoiding. Don't worry- it's not as complicated as you might think. Find out in the next chapter.

Chapter 2: Keto eating: What's ON the Menu and What's NOT

You've been desperate to get to this chapter for the whole start of this book, haven't you? Here I've been, telling you about the benefits and the background and all you could think about was food. Right?

Yeah, I can completely get where you're coming from on that. Because I LOVE food too.

Life wouldn't be living if I couldn't regularly chow down on Mexican food, burgers, raspberry fat bombs and cake.

So, let me reassure you that you *can* eat all these tasty meals on the Keto diet, you don't need to go crazy with portion control and you don't have to nibble lettuce leaves. Yes, you do need to make a few habit adjustments but that's about it. Nothing too complicated at all.

Let me show you more about your brand new Keto menu....

Here's what's ON the menu

These are the foods you can keep right on eating on the Keto diet.

Meat, poultry, game, fish and seafood

Fill up your plate and tuck right in to as much meat as you like on the Keto diet. As far as possible, choose organic, grass-fed and hormone-free to ensure you're giving your body the best quality nutrition possible. Make sure you avoid processed meats, battered fish and meats coated in breadcrumbs. Yum!

Choose from any of the following:

- Beef
- Pork
- Lamb
- Game
- Goat
- Chicken
- Turkey
- Organ meats

- Salmon
- Mackerel
- Sardines
- Herring
- Cod

Eggs

Yep, you can keep on eating eggs on the Keto diet. In fact, they work absolutely brilliantly when you start meal-prepping, so I'd highly advise you to include plenty. They're also rich in a wide range of nutrients including B-vitamins, iron, protein, and disease-fighting nutrients like lutein and zeaxanthin. Enjoy!

Dairy

One of my favorite things about the Keto diet is the fact you can still indulge in those mouth-watering foods like butter, sour cream, cheese and yoghurt completely guilt-free. Better still, you don't need to opt for zero-fat, zero-taste versions either.

Having said that, it's best to go careful if you choose to drink milk as it contains a high amount of lactose (a type of sugar). You don't want to undo all your hard work with a drink, do you?

Fats, oils and sauces

As you've guessed by reading that last part about dairy, you don't have to limit fat whatsoever on the Keto diet.

However, it's best to stick to wholefood sources of fat such as butter, cream, olive oil and coconut oil, and avoid trans fats and polyunsaturated vegetable oils. These are high in omega 6, which has been linked to heart disease and many inflammatory diseases.

Enjoy these:

- Butter
- Cream
- Coconut oil
- Olive oil
- Ghee
- Chicken fat
- Avocados
- Mayonnaise
- High-fat sauces

Vegetables

Yes! You can keep eating plenty of veggies on the Keto diet. And indeed, you should so you can keep plenty of vitamins, minerals and antioxidants as possible filling up your body. But choose carefully- many of the usual go-to veggies are contain quite substantial carbs. Choose these instead:

- Green leafy veggies like kale, collards, Bok choy & spinach
- Cauliflower
- Broccoli
- Cabbage
- Brussels sprouts
- Asparagus
- Zucchini
- Eggplant
- Olives
- Mushrooms
- Cucumber
- Lettuce
- Avocado
- Onions
- Garlic

Herbs and spices

You can keep enjoying as many fresh or dried herbs and spices as your heart desires on the Keto diet. Just make sure you choose 100% sugar-free, gluten-free dried spices (you'd be surprised what they put in- check the labels). Mmmm... my mouth is watering at the thought of lightly toasted cumin seeds, fresh fragrant cilantro and more...

Sauces and condiments

Even though most of sauces you'll find in the store are high in sugars, you'll still find plenty of lovely extras you can add to your diet when you eat Keto. Try some of these for size:

- Soy sauce
- Lemon juice
- Lime juice
- Sriracha sauce

- Tabasco and Red-Hot sauce (check the label)
- Vinegar: white, cider and red wine
- Homemade mayo
- Dijon mustard
- Wholegrain mustard (but check the label)
- Hot sauces (but check the label)
- Salad dressings (homemade only)

Sweeteners

Whilst artificial sweeteners aren't entirely zero carb, and they're not exactly healthy either, they can be a useful way to add some sweetness to your diet without going crazy on the carbs.

You can choose from:

- Erythritol
- Stevia
- Splenda
- Brand-name sugar replacements

Some purists say that sweeteners should be completely off the menu- that's for you to decide.

Alcohol

Yes, you can drink the occasional glass of something grown-up on the Keto diet. Just make sure you don't overdo it (alcohol is high carb) and choose your drinks wisely.

Avoid cocktails, high-sugar lagers, spirits with soda as the mixer (such as brandy and coke).

Better choices include champagne, red or white wine, pure spirits like whiskey, tequila, vodka, Dry Martini, and brand. If you do need a mixer, opt for sparkling water.

Non-Alcoholic Drinks

Quench your thirst with something other than high-sugar soda and juice, and instead stick with something cheap, easy and delicious. Tea, coffee and plain water are all great. Make sure you're avoiding those syrups and sugars if you opt for 'fancy' coffee, though. Again, it's another way those carbs often sneak in!

Snacks

You don't need to quick snacking when you go Keto, but you DO need to choose carefully. Here are my favorite options:

- Celery with nut butter
- Nuts and seeds (not cashew nuts)
- Hard-boiled eggs
- Bacon rashers
- Ham Roll-Ups (filled with avocado and cucumber or scrambled eggs)
- Sliced cucumber, avocado and celery
- Sauerkraut and Kimchi
- Pork rinds and crackling
- Fat bombs

Here's what's OFF the menu

By now you should be feeling excited about the Keto diet, and perhaps even excited about the possibility of eating those mouth-watering foods. I know I was.

Now let's turn to the slightly *less* fun bit. I'll guide you through the foods you need to avoid when you follow Keto.

Sugar

Sugars and carbs are the same thing, so stop eating them in all their forms! Yes, I know it's easier said than done, but it will be well worth it.

Don't feel like you have to throw yourself into Keto straight away. You can start by ditching the sugar in your morning coffee, avoiding processed foods and cooking for yourself more often.

Also avoid:

- Soft drinks
- Fruit yoghurts
- Premade cereal bars
- Smoothies
- Candy
- Juice
- Sports drinks
- Chocolate
- Cake

- Buns
- Pastries
- Ice cream
- Donuts
- Cookies
- Breakfast cereals

Carbs and grains

I don't need to preach to the converted, do I? These are all high carb. Avoid them and products made from them.

- Wheat
- Barley
- Oats
- Rice
- Rye
- Corn
- Quinoa
- Millet
- Sorghum
- Bulgur
- Amaranth
- Sprouted grains
- Buckwheat

This includes foods made from these ingredients, (wholegrain, whole-meal, brown, white and corn) which include:

- Bread
- Pasta
- Rice
- Potatoes
- French fries
- Potato chips
- Porridge
- Oats
- Muesli

Beans & Lentils

Sorry vegetarians, vegans and chili-lovers. Beans and lentils are high carb, so you'll need to ditch them. Yes, that includes:

- Red, green, brown and black lentils
- Red Kidney beans
- Black-Eye beans
- Chickpeas
- Black beans
- Green peas
- Lima beans
- Pinto beans
- White beans
- Fava beans

Fruit

Fruit is high in natural sugars which have a similar effect on your body as the processed white stuff. You'll need to avoid fruit juice, dried fruit and smoothies too. Berries are OK in small quantities, but exercise caution.

Occasionally I'll share recipes in this book which do contain a small amount of fruit which contain carbs. This is usually less than 1g per serving so it's up to you whether to indulge or skip.

Hopefully you're not feeling too overwhelmed by all this information. As I said at the start of the chapter, you really don't have to surrender too many of your favorite foods to succeed with the Keto diet. With a few tweaks you can keep creating your favorite dishes, but with none of the fattening, health-damaging side effects.

Now we've covered the Keto diet, let's turn our attention to the lifehack that brought you to this book in the first place- Meal Prep!

Turn to the next chapter where I'll explain everything you need to know as well as sharing plenty of handy hints that will help you make meal prep work for you.

Chapter 3: What is Meal Prepping?

Meal prep is the practice of pre-preparing your foods before they're to be eaten.

You store them in the fridge or freezer until you're ready to eat them, and then you enjoy them.

Easy!

There's nothing complicated about this stuff. There's nothing fancy or high tech about it. It's just good common sense, great organization and your food will taste even better!

You've probably done it many times before, but never realized that you were doing meal prep.

For example, your mother was doing meal prep for you when she packed you off to school with sandwiches, a bento box or another container full of nourishing treats to fuel you through the day.

You do it every time you have leftovers from a meal and put them into the fridge to eat the following day. You even do it when you bake some kind of treat (pancakes, cookies or cake anyone?) but don't eat the whole thing.

Even though it's nothing amazing, it will have an amazing effect on your life if you start meal prepping on a regular basis.

→ Meal prep your breakfasts and you'll know that you have something decent to fill your stomach before you head out to work in the morning.

→ Meal prep your lunch and you'll save dollars spent on takeaway junk that probably doesn't fit your Keto lifestyle anyway.

→ Meal prep your dinners and you can save your energy and just grab your meal from the fridge and flop onto the couch, instead of slaving away in the kitchen.

If you're working on a side hustle, you'll rescue much-needed hours that you could be spending on your business. You'll get to spend more time with your partner or the kids. You'll find time to read that novel, or take up a new hobby, or to get more stuff done...

Meal prep really is amazing!

Why meal prep foods for the Keto diet?

The Keto diet is perfectly suited for meal prep because most of the food you'll be making will store perfectly. The flavors will deepen, the meats will become even tenderer, the sauces will thicken, and those sweet treats will REALLY taste good.

As we all know, the Keto diet isn't the easiest in the world to follow, especially if you're living a busy lifestyle. It's not always easy to find grain-free alternatives or healthy food that doesn't involve high-carb veggies and fruit. You often have to accept whatever there is on offer.

Not so when you do meal prep. Because you can perfectly control what you're eating, you can control the portion size (so keep a closer eye on your macros) and you can keep your costs down too.

Everything is perfectly planned, so you can use everything in the fridge without needing to see a scrap of food go to waste. What more could you want for your healthy lifestyle?

How to Meal Prep

The beauty about meal prep is that everyone has his or her own way of doing it.

Everyone has their own favorite foods, their own appetite to consider and their own lifestyle to take into account.

However, there are a few tips I can share with you on how to get started and how to make Keto meal prep work for you.

#1: Pick your day
Most people choose a day to do the majority of their meal prep. It just works better when you can get into the kitchen and get stuff done.

Sunday is a good day because you're more likely to be around with time to spare. Wednesdays also work well because it's midway through the week.

Which day works best for you?

#2: Pick a meal
Which meal would you like to focus on first?

Are breakfasts a nightmare for you? Are you sick of making dinner every night when you get home when you've got so much to do? Maybe your lunchbox could do with an overhaul? Or maybe, even, you need to get working on your snack foods....

If you've been meal prepping for a while, you might decide to be adventurous and try meal prepping two meals per day or even three.

What will you be doing?

#3: What will you be eating?

Now you get to decide exactly what you want to eat! This part should be both easy and fun because I've packed plenty of delicious meals and snacks into the book to get you started, so have a look through and see what takes your fancy.

Remember, nutritionally speaking it's a good idea to keep some variety in your meals. It's also a sure way to beat the boredom. So, select a few recipes to try and alternate them over the course of a week.

I've organized the recipes here under certain headings to make it easier for you to find them, but, as I said earlier on, that doesn't mean that you're tied into eating them at these times of day. If you want to eat blueberry cake for dinner and chicken fajitas for breakfast, then DO IT!

It's your body, your lifestyle and your happiness.

For best nutrition and taste, it's good to follow this formula when you're creating your meals:

Healthy protein + healthy grain (or grain alternative) + vegetables or fruit + healthy fat.

#4: Make your plan

Now grab some paper and a pen and write down exactly what you'll be eating. You can use a blank calendar for this or even your computer if you prefer. Don't skip this step- it will help you stay on track!

#5: Find a healthy storage box

You can use pretty much any kind of storage container you like for your meal prep- just grab whatever you have and throw the ingredients inside. It's better for the planet and it's better for your bank balance too.

If you don't have anything lying around at home, it's worth taking time to think about what works best before you invest. Here are my top tips for brilliant storage containers:

1) **Find one that is divided into sections.** It will help keep food separate.
2) **Make sure it's airtight-** Airtight means your food will stay fresh for longer.

3) **Free from BPAs-** BPAs are harmful for your health as they can release estrogen-like compounds which interfere with your natural hormone production. Yes, even if you're a guy. Watch out for plastic symbol #7 and avoid it like the plague!!

4) **Is it microwavable?** If you're using plastic, it's not such a great idea to reheat food. But if you're using glass, it can be a really useful feature.

5) **Can you see what's inside?** - OMG, the number of times I've pulled something from my fridge of freezer and I haven't had a clue what's inside. Don't make my mistakes. Find one you can see through and that you can label.

6) **Are they the same size?** It's much easier to portion out your meals if you have the same size boxes. Better still if you can stack them.

#6: Write your shopping list and hit the store!

Now you know what you're cooking you can work out what you need to buy. I'd highly recommend that you do it 'old-style' and scribble your list on a scrap piece of paper. Then you can get in and out fast, you know you have exactly what you need, and you won't waste time or money.

#7: Get prepping!

Now comes the fun part! The meal prep!

Get into that kitchen and do whatever you need to do to create delicious meals you can grab whenever you're hungry. You'll probably need to a ton of peeling, chopping, sautéing, baking and stirring, but it will all be worth it in the end.

Why not listen to your favorite music whilst you're cooking to help pass the time faster? Or listen to a podcast, learn a new language or just get mindful and enjoy what you're doing.

Bear in mind that you don't have to prep absolutely everything in your meal beforehand. Foods like avocados are much better sliced just before eating. Lettuce leaves will go soggy if you leave them hanging around too long. Simply package them together and assemble when needed.

Meal prep doesn't have to involve cooking beforehand either. You can always portion up the ingredients you need for each meal, pop into zip lock bags or containers and use when needed. In my opinion, this works very well for salads and stir fries, but not so well when it comes to cooked dishes. As ever, it's up to you what approach you decide to take.

#7: Don't quit

When you start doing meal prep, it can all seem overwhelming. You might not want to dedicate a couple of hours every Sunday to cooking. You might feel confused about everything you need to get done.

But don't quit! Like anything, the more you practice, the better you'll become. You can tweak everything to your likes and dislikes and make your Keto meal prep the best lifestyle hack you've ever discovered.

So now you're clued up about the diet, you know how to make meal prep work for you. Let's get on to the recipes!

Chapter 4: Ketogenic Meal Prep Recipes
Breakfast

Sausage and Egg Breakfast Sandwich

Eggs make the perfect Keto meal prep breakfast. But that doesn't mean they have to be repetitive or boring. Check out these mouth-watering breakfast sandwiches, and you'll never look at eggs in the same way again!

Serves: 4

Time: 10 minutes

- Calories: 603
- Net Carbs 4g
- Protein: 22g
- Fat: 54g

Ingredients:

- 4 Tbsp. butter
- 8 large eggs
- 4 Tbsp. mayonnaise
- 8 sausage patties, cooked
- 8 slices sharp cheddar cheese
- Sliced avocado, to taste

Method:

1. Pop the butter into a skillet and place over a warm heat.
2. Add silicon egg molds, crack the eggs inside and gently whisk the eggs.
3. Cover and cook for 3-4 mins.
4. Remove the eggs from the rings.
5. Place one egg on a plate, cover with 1/8 mayo, followed by a sausage patty, a slice of cheese and some avocado.
6. Add the next sausage patty and top with the cheese.
7. Spread another 1/8 of the mayo over another egg and use this to top the sandwich.
8. Repeat with the remaining ingredients.
9. You can either serve and enjoy this right away or divide into containers and pop into the fridge. Don't assemble until right before you're ready to eat.

Avocado Egg Breakfast

It can be hard to know how to serve your eggs when bread is off the menu. I know, I've been there. Enter the magnificent avocado bowl. Creamy, rich and amazing, you'll fall in love with them.

Serves: 3
Time: 20 mins

- Calories: 500
- Net carbs: 3g
- Protein: 25g
- Fat: 40g

Ingredients:

- 3 avocados
- 3 Tbsp. salted butter
- 9 free-range eggs
- 9 rashers bacon, cut into small pieces
- Pinch of salt and black pepper

Method:

1. Place a large skillet over a medium heat and add around half the butter.
2. Take a medium bowl and whisk the eggs together with the salt and pepper.
3. Pour into the pan and cook, stirring often to scramble.
4. Take another skillet, add the rest of the butter and cook the bacon.
5. Remove from the heat.
6. Crumble the bacon into the eggs and stir well to combine, then allow to cool completely.
7. Divide between storage containers and pop into the fridge until needed.
8. On serving day, slice open the avocado, remove the stone and fill with the egg and bacon mixture (you might want to reheat first). Then enjoy!

Breakfast Pumpkin Bread

Yes, you can have cake for breakfast. And not only will it taste awesome, it's perfectly Keto and utterly moreish. Yum!

Serves: 4

Time: 55 mins (approx.)

- Calories: 105
- Net carbs: 1.55g
- Protein: 0.3g
- Fat: 10.3g

Ingredients:

For the bread...

- 6 free-range eggs
- ½ coconut oil, melted
- 2 Tbsp. butter
- 1 cup pumpkin puree
- 4 tsp. pumpkin pie spice
- 2 Tbsp. sour cream
- 1 ½ cups powdered sweetener
- 2 tsp. vanilla
- ½ cup + 2 tablespoons coconut flour
- ½ tsp. salt
- 1 ½ tsp. baking powder

For the icing...

- 2 Tbsp. powdered sweetener
- 2 tsp. melted butter
- 2 tsp. heavy whipping cream

Method:

1. Grease 4 mini loaf tins and line with parchment paper, and preheat the oven to 350°F.
2. Melt the coconut oil and butter together. Pop to one side.
3. Grab a large bowl and combine the eggs, sweetener, pumpkin puree, sour cream, vanilla and spice. Stir well.
4. Gently add the coconut oil mixture and stir though.
5. Take another bowl and add the coconut flour, salt and baking powder. Stir well.
6. Pour the flour mixture into the wet ingredients and stir.
7. Pour into the pre-prepared tins and bake for 45 minutes until cooked through.
8. Remove from the oven and allow to cool whilst preparing the icing.

9. Grab a pan and add the butter and sweetener. Melt over a low heat. Add the cream and stir well.
10. Pour over the bread and allow to cool completely.
11. Pop into zip lock bags and store in a cool dry place, or in the freezer until needed.

Stuffed Breakfast Biscuits

For an instant, tasty breakfast, why not create these clever treats. They include all the macros you need in a breakfast, you can reheat them perfectly in a few seconds and they taste incredible. Enjoy!

Serves: 6

Time: 20 mins

- Calories: 250
- Net carbs: 2g
- Protein: 12g
- Fat: 20g

Ingredients:

- 2 oz. cream cheese
- 2 cups mozzarella, shredded
- 2 free-range eggs, beaten
- 1 cup almond flour
- Pinch salt & pepper
- 2 oz. cheese, cubed
- 6 breakfast sausage patties, pre-cooked

Method:

1. Start by preheating your oven to 400°F and grease a muffin tin.
2. Next grab a microwave bowl and add the cream cheese and mozzarella. Pop into the microwave for 30 seconds until the cheese is soft and mix well to combine.
3. Grab another bowl and add the almond flour and egg. Stir well to combine.
4. Add the cheese to the almond flour mixture, stir well again and then pop into some plastic wrap. Place into the fridge for an hour to firm up.
5. Remove from the fridge and cut into six slices.
6. Flatten the slices, pop a sausage patty onto each slice, top with the cheese, and wrap the sides of the dough around the meat and cheese.
7. Pop into the oven for 12-15 minutes.
8. Remove from the oven and allow to cool completely before storing in a storage box until needed.

Italian Breakfast Casserole

For a grab-and-go breakfast that tastes amazing, take a few minutes to create this amazing breakfast casserole. You can experiment by switching the sausage for something spicy, add some healthy greens or pile in the cheese to make it really something special.

Serves: 4

Time: 40 mins

- Calories: 859
- Net carbs: 5g
- Protein: 34g
- Fat: 78g

Ingredients:

- 7 oz. cauliflower, chopped into bite-sized pieces
- 12 oz. Italian sausage
- 2 oz. butter
- 8 free-range eggs
- 1 cup heavy whipping cream
- 5 oz. shredded cheese
- ¼ cup fresh basil
- Salt and pepper, to taste

Method:

1. Start by preheating the oven to 400°F and grease a casserole dish.
2. Place the butter into the skillet, pop over a medium heat and fry the cauliflower until soft.
3. Next add the sausage and cook through.
4. Grab a medium bowl and combine the remaining ingredients (except the basil). Stir well to combine.
5. Next place the sausage and cauliflower into the casserole dish, pour the egg over the top and stir well to combine.
6. Pop into the oven and cook for 30-40 minutes.
7. Remove from the oven and allow to cool completely.
8. Divide into portions and pop into storage containers. Place into the fridge and store until needed.

Overnight Chia Oatmeal

You know those days when you REALLY miss oatmeal? When you'd do anything just to dig into a bowl of warm, filling porridge and let it give you a huge from the inside? I thought you'd say that. Which is why I've created this Keto version. It makes enough to feed two hungry people, but you can always double the batch if you need more. You can also warm this up if you prefer.

Serves: 2

Time: 10 mins

- Calories: 171
- Net carbs: 4.8g
- Protein: 2.3g
- Fat: 16.5g

Ingredients:

- ½ cup chia seeds
- ¼ cup unsweetened shredded coconut
- ¼ tsp. vanilla
- ½ cup coconut milk
- 1 cup almond milk
- 2 Tbsp. stevia
- 1/8 tsp. pumpkin spice seasoning
- 1/8 tsp. cinnamon

Method:

1. This is the easiest breakfast in the world! Simply place the ingredients into a storage container and stir well.
2. Cover and pop in the fridge.
3. Once soaked overnight, you can divide this into portions to last you for several days. It will keep well in the fridge for several days.

Blueberry Bread

Blueberries are a wonderful fruit for the Keto diet. They hit the spot when it comes to sweetness without being too high carb. They really pack a punch when it comes to antioxidants and they keep your nutrient count super-high. Enjoy!

Serves: 12

Time: 1 ½ hours

- Calories: 169
- Net carbs: 5.2g
- Protein: 7.4g
- Fat: 11g

Ingredients:

For the bread...

- 6 free-range eggs
- 9 Tbsp. melted butter
- ¾ cup fresh blueberries
- ½ tsp. cinnamon
- 2 Tbsp. sour cream
- 2/3 cup granulated sweetener
- 1 ½ tsp. vanilla
- 2 Tbsp. heavy whipping cream
- ½ cup + 2 Tbsp. coconut flour
- ½ tsp. salt
- 1 ½ tsp. baking powder

For the icing...

- 2 Tbsp. powdered sweetener
- 1 tsp. butter, melted
- 1 tsp. heavy whipping cream
- Dash of vanilla
- ¼ tsp. lemon zest

Method:

1. Grease and line a loaf tin and preheat the oven to 350°F.
2. Next melt the butter and beat in the sweetener, sour cream, heavy whipping cream, eggs, vanilla, salt, baking powder and cinnamon. Mix until combined.
3. Then add the ½ cup flour and mix well.
4. Grab another bowl and pop the blueberries inside, with the extra coconut flour. Stir to coat then throw into the batter.
5. Stir well and pour into the baking tin.

6. Bake for 65-75 mins until cooked through, then leave to cool.
7. Meanwhile, make the icing by whisking together the icing ingredients. Drizzle over your cake.
8. Slice into portions and pop into zip lock bags until ready to enjoy!

Greek Egg Bake

For those of you with more savory tastes in the morning, get your mouth around this egg bake. Pimped with salty, chewy sundried tomatoes, tender cheese and nutrient-dense kale, you'll tick those nutritional boxes and start your day the right way.

Serves: 6

Time: 25 mins

- Calories: 175
- Net carbs: 5g
- Protein: 15g
- Fat: 11g

Ingredients:

- 12 free-range eggs
- 1 cup kale, chopped
- ¼ cup sundried tomatoes
- ½ cup feta cheese
- ½ tsp. oregano
- Salt and pepper, to taste

Method:

1. Line a pan with foil and grease well, then preheat the oven to 350°F.
2. Grab a large bowl and whisk together the eggs.
3. Throw in the kale, tomatoes, feta and seasonings and stir again to combine.
4. Pour into the pan and pop into the oven for 25 mins until cooked through.
5. Remove from the oven and allow to cool.
6. Slice into portions and pop into zip lock bags for the week.

Turmeric Scrambled Eggs

Want to kick-start your day with something epic, both in the taste department and when it comes to nutrients too? Then try these turmeric scrambled eggs! Turmeric is a superfood which is rich in antioxidants, cancer-fighting substances and it even keeps your brain working efficiently. Enjoy with veggies and sausages for best results!

Serves: 2

Time: 5 mins

- Calories: 1400
- Net carbs: 6g
- Protein: 29g
- Fat: 18g

Ingredients:

- 4 free-range eggs
- 2 Tbsp. milk
- 2 tsp. dried turmeric
- ½ tsp. dried parsley
- Salt and pepper, to taste
- 1 cup broccoli, steamed
- 8 small sausages, pre-cooked

Method:

1. Place some oil into a skillet and pop over a medium heat.
2. Grab a bowl and whisk the eggs, milk, turmeric, parsley and salt and pepper together.
3. Pour the eggs into the pan and stir well as it cooks. This should only take 2-3 minutes.
4. Flip the whole thing over and cook for another 2-3 mins.
5. Remove from the heat and allow to cool.
6. Divide into two containers, add the broccoli and sausages, and pop the lid on.
7. Store until needed.

Cauliflower Hash Browns

My mother used to serve up hash browns every Sunday morning when we were kids, and if I'm honest, I LOVED their greasy, potato-ey texture. I really missed them when I started Keto. Then someone passed me this recipe and said, 'Go make them!' and the rest is history.

Serves: 6

Time: 45 mins

- Calories: 164
- Net carbs: 3.2g
- Protein: 7g
- Fat: 11.25g

Ingredients:

- 1 small head grated cauliflower (about 3 cups)
- 1 free-range egg
- ¾ cup shredded cheddar cheese
- ¼ tsp. cayenne pepper (opt.)
- ¼ tsp. garlic powder
- ½ tsp. salt
- 1/8 tsp. black pepper

Method:

1. Preheat your oven to 400°F and grease a baking tray.
2. Then grate the head of cauliflower, pop into a bowl and microwave for 3 minutes. Allow to cool.
3. Place into a clean tea towel and press out the excess moisture, then place into a bowl.
4. Add the remaining ingredients to the bowl and stir well to combine.
5. Shape into six and pop onto the baking tray, then cook for 15- 20 mins.
6. Remove from the oven, cool and pop into storage containers until needed.

Blueberry Pancake Bites

Mmmm... you gotta love pancakes for breakfast! These are perfectly sweet, the flavor is well-rounded and the coconut flour lifts them from average to awesome. I'd eat them every day if I could! Enjoy!

Serves: 24
Time: 40 mins

- Calories: 188
- Net carbs: 3.7g
- Protein: 5.7g
- Fat: 13g

Ingredients:

- 4 free-range eggs
- ¼ cup sweetener
- ½ tsp. vanilla extract
- ½ cup coconut flour
- ¼ cup butter
- 1 tsp. baking powder
- ½ tsp. salt
- ¼ tsp. cinnamon
- 1/3 to ½ cup water
- ½ cup frozen wild blueberries

Method:

1. Start by preheating your oven to 325°F and greasing a mini muffin tray.
2. Next place the eggs, sweetener and vanilla into a blender and blend until smooth.
3. Add the coconut flour, melted butter, baking powder, salt and cinnamon. Blend again until smooth.
4. Add 1/3 cup water and blend again, then leave to sit for 5 minutes to thicken up. If it's too thick, add the remaining water and blend again. It should be thick enough to scoop.
5. Pour into the muffin cups, add a few blueberries and then pop into the oven.
6. Bake for 20-25 mins, then remove and allow to cool.
7. Pop into zip lock bags until needed.

Sausage Ball Puffs

These gorgeous little puffs are a revelation. I eat them for breakfast, I happily snack on them all day long, and I love to serve them up at parties when no one has a clue they're eating Keto. The smiles say it all. Get cooking and you'll see.

Serves: 36

Time: 25 mins

- Calories: 89
- Net carbs: 0.3g
- Protein: 4g
- Fat: 7g

Ingredients:

- 1 lb. breakfast sausage, browned and drained
- 4 ½ Tbsp. butter, melted and cooled
- 1/3 cup coconut flour
- 2 Tbsp. sour cream
- 4 free-range eggs
- ¼ tsp. salt
- ¼ tsp. baking powder
- 2 cups sharp shredded cheddar cheese

Method:

1. Grease a baking tray and preheat your oven to 375°F.
2. Next grab a bowl and combine the melted butter, eggs, salt and sour cream. Whisk well until combined.
3. Add the coconut flour and baking powder and stir until combined.
4. Add the sausage, and the cheese and stir again until combined.
5. Drop spoonfuls of this batter on the baking tray then pop into the oven.
6. Cook for 15-18 minus until brown.
7. Remove from the oven, cool and store in zip lock bags until ready to be enjoyed.

Acai Almond Butter Smoothie

Yes! Being on Keto doesn't mean you have to sacrifice your morning smoothies either. Just switch those high carb fruits with low carb berries, pile in the protein and you're good to go. Again, double up the quantities if you want to make more.

Serves: 1-2

Time: 5 mins

- Calories: 345
- Net carbs: 6g
- Protein: 15g
- Fat: 20g

Ingredients:

- 1 x 4 oz. pack unsweetened Acai puree
- ¾ cup unsweetened almond milk
- ¼ avocado
- 3 Tbsp. protein powder
- 1 Tbsp. coconut oil
- 1 Tbsp. almond butter
- ½ tsp. vanilla extract
- 2 drops liquid stevia (opt.)

Method:

1. Throw all ingredients into your blender, hit that whizz button and blend until smooth.
2. Divide between storage containers and store until needed.
3. Consume within a day or so.

Cauliflower and Ground Beef Omelet

Sick of eggs, bacon and sausage? Then you'll love this amazing beef omelet. It's unusual, surprisingly tasty and perfect for fueling your morning workouts.

Serves: 4

Time: 45 mins

- Calories: 544
- Net carbs: 8g
- Protein: 20g
- Fat: 48g

Ingredients:

- 2 Tbsp. ghee
- ½ small onion, chopped
- 2 cloves garlic, chopped
- 4 jalapeño peppers, sliced
- 1 lb. ground beef
- 1 tsp. Himalayan salt
- ½ tsp. freshly cracked black pepper
- 1 small head cauliflower, grated
- ½ cup paleo mayo
- ½ cup water
- ¼ cup toasted sunflower seed butter
- 1 Tbsp. coconut aminos
- 1 tsp. fish sauce
- 1 tsp. ground cumin
- 4 free-range eggs
- 2 jalapeño peppers, sliced
- ½ ripe avocado, diced
- 2 Tbsp. paleo mayo
- 1 Tbsp. Apple Cider vinegar
- 1 Tbsp. fresh parsley, chopped

Method:

1. Start by placing the ghee into a skillet and pop over a medium heat.
2. Add the onion, garlic and jalapeño and cook for 5 minutes.
3. Add the beef, season well and brown.
4. Add the cauliflower and cook for a further 5 minutes.
5. Grab a small bowl and add the mayo, water, sunflower seed butter, coconut aminos, fish sauce and cumin. Stir well to combine.

6. Pour this sauce over the beef and cauliflower and stir again. Cook for a further 5 minutes.
7. Make four small holes in the top and add the eggs, then broil for 10 minutes until cooked.
8. Whilst this is cooking, place the mayo and the apple cider vinegar into a bowl and combine.
9. Pour over the skillet, sprinkle with parsley and leave to cool completely.
10. Divide between storage containers and store in the fridge until needed.

Ultimate Keto Bagels

I know what you're thinking. You're thinking, 'But...bagels can't be Keto. Can they?'. And yes, they absolutely can. Ask our friend almond flour to help, add lashings of flavorings and whip them together with omega-3 rich eggs and you have a breakfast to remember.

Serves: 6

Time: 15 mins

- Calories: 360
- Net carbs: 5g
- Protein: 21g
- Fat: 28g

Ingredients:

- 2 cups almond flour
- 1 Tbsp. baking powder
- 1 tsp. garlic powder
- 1 tsp. onion powder
- 1 tsp. dried Italian seasoning
- 3 free-range eggs, divided
- 3 cups shredded mozzarella cheese
- 5 Tbsp. cream cheese
- 1 Tbsp. sesame seeds
- 1 tsp. poppy seeds
- 1 Tbsp. dried onion flakes
- 1 Tbsp. dried garlic flakes
- ½ tsp. salt

[handwritten note: OR Everything Bagel Spice]

Method:

1. Start by preheating the oven to 425°F and grease and line a baking tray.
2. Grab a large bowl and add the almond flour, baking powder, garlic powder, onion powder and Italian seasoning. Mix until combined.
3. Take a small bowl and crack an egg inside. Whisk well, then pop to one side.
4. Next take a microwavable bowl and mix together the mozzarella cheese and cream cheese. Microwave for 1-2 minutes until soft. Stir well.
5. Cool slightly then add the remaining eggs, plus the almond flour mixture. Mix well until combined.
6. Divide into then roll each into a ball. Shape gently into a ring, pressing your finger into the middle to make the hole.
7. Place onto the baking tray, brush with the egg wash, and cook for 12-15 minutes.
8. Remove and cool before slicing and storing until needed.

Blackberry Egg Bake

This wonderful egg bake is partly like one of those mouth-watering desserts your mother used to make, tweaked with the taste of fresh rosemary and orange, and whipped up into a package which is great for breakfast (or snacks, or whenever you need a sweet, low-carb fix).

Serves: 4
Time: 20 mins

- Calories: 144
- Net carbs: 2g
- Protein: 8.5g
- Fat: 10g

Ingredients:

- 5 free-range eggs
- 1 Tbsp. butter, melted
- 3 Tbsp. coconut flour
- 1 tsp. grated fresh ginger
- ¼ tsp. vanilla
- 1/3 tsp. fine sea salt
- Zest of ½ orange
- 1 tsp. fresh rosemary, chopped
- ½ cup fresh blackberries (plus a few extra for topping)

Method:

1. Start by preheating the oven to 350°F and grease four ramekins.
2. Grab your blender and add all the ingredients, except the rosemary and blackberries. Whizz until smooth.
3. Add the rosemary and blackberries and whizz for a second or two until chopped.
4. Pour between the ramekins and top with a few extra, then pop into the oven.
5. Cook for 20 minutes.
6. Remove and allow to cool, before storing until needed.

Cauliflower Fritters

These gorgeous little fritters are packed with omega 3s, B-complex vitamins and a ton of health protein that will keep you feeling amazing all morning long. They're cheesy, they're tender, and one is never enough.

Serves: 6
Time: 30 mins

- Calories: 60
- Net carbs: 0.7g
- Protein: 2g
- Fat: 5g

Ingredients:

- 1 large head of cauliflower, broken into florets
- 2 free-range eggs
- 2/3 cup almond flour
- 1 Tbsp. nutritional yeast
- ½ tsp. turmeric
- ½ tsp. sea salt
- ¼ tsp. black pepper
- 1-2 Tbsp. ghee

Method:

1. First boil the cauliflower in a large pot of water for 10 minutes then place in the food processor.
2. Whizz until chopped finely.
3. Pour into a medium bowl and add the eggs, flour, yeast, turmeric, salt and pepper. Stir well to combine.
4. Form into 6 patties.
5. Place some of the ghee into a skillet, pop over a medium heat and cook as many of the fritters as you can fit into the pan. Repeat with the rest of the fritters.
6. Remove from the pan and allow to cool, then pop into storage containers.
7. Store in the fridge until needed.

Lunch

White Turkey Chili

If you've never tried turkey chili before, you're in for a real treat. Perfect for using up leftover turkey, packed with amino-acids and completely yummy, you'll get all the taste but with none of the traditional chili carbs. Enjoy!

Serves: 3
Time: 20 minutes

- Calories: 388
- Net carbs: 5.5g
- Protein: 28g
- Fat: 30.5g

Ingredients

- 1 lb. ground turkey
- 2 cups riced cauliflower
- 2 Tbsp. coconut oil
- ½ white onion
- 2 garlic cloves
- 2 cups full fat coconut milk (or heavy cream)
- 1 Tbsp. mustard
- 1 tsp. salt
- 1 tsp. black pepper
- 1 tsp. dried thyme
- 1 tsp. celery salt
- 1 tsp. garlic powder
- Chili flakes, to taste

Method:

1. Place the coconut oil in a large pan, pop over a medium heat and cook the onion and garlic.
2. Add the turkey and cook for a further minute or so before adding the seasonings and the cauliflower.
3. Stir well and cook until brown.
4. Add the coconut milk, simmer and cook for a further 10 minutes.
5. Leave to cool completely then divide into storage containers.
6. Store until needed.

Curry Chicken Lettuce Wraps

If you're like me and your second-favorite food in the whole world is curry (it's spicy, isn't it?!), then you'll love making these wraps a regular lunchtime feature. Be sure not to wrap them to far in advance before serving- you'll just end up with soggy leaves, which isn't such a pleasant food for lunchtime.

Serves: 2

Time: 20 mins

- Calories: 544
- Net carbs: 7.2g
- Protein: 50.9g
- Fat: 36.4g

Ingredients:

- 1 lb. boneless skinless chicken thighs
- ¼ cup minced onion
- 2 cloves garlic, minced
- 2 tsp. curry powder
- 1 ½ tsp. salt
- 1 tsp. black pepper
- 3 Tbsp. butter or ghee
- 1 cup cauliflower rice
- 6-8 small lettuce leaves
- ¼ cup coconut milk

Method:

1. Pop a skillet over a medium heat, add half the butter or ghee and cook the onion until sort.
2. Next add the chicken, garlic and salt. Cook for 10 minutes until brown.
3. Add the rest of the ghee, the curry and the cauliflower rice. Stir until combined, then remove from the heat.
4. Allow to cool completely and divide into storage containers, with the lettuce and coconut cream.
5. On serving day, pile the chicken mixture into the lettuce, top with the cream and then enjoy!

Cheddar-Wrapped Taco Rolls

Since I tried these cheese tacos, I've become a convert! I mean, how can regular tacos ever compare when you have food like this??? You can either do as I have and create everything together, or make the shell, cook the meat and throw it all together when you're ready to eat. You decide!

Serves: 4

Time: 30 mins

- Calories: 491
- Net carbs: 2g
- Protein: 37g
- Fat: 35g

Ingredients:

For the crust...

- 2 cups cheddar cheese

For the toppings...

- 1 cup taco meat (cooked and seasoned ahead of time)
- ¼ cup tomatoes, chopped
- ½ avocado, chopped
- 2 tsp. Sriracha sauce

Method:

1. Start by greasing and lining a baking tray and preheating your oven to 400°F.
2. Spread the cheese over the baking sheet thinly, and pop into the oven to bake for 15 minutes.
3. Remove from the oven and try to use a spatula to lift from the baking sheet. If it doesn't work, pop back into the oven.
4. Next add the taco meat and pop back into the oven for 5-10 mins.
5. As this is cooking, combine the remaining toppings in a bowl.
6. Remove the pizza from the oven then top with the remaining toppings.
7. Use a large knife or a pizza cutter to divide into four slices and roll in on itself to create tacos.
8. Allow to cool completely before storing in storage containers or a zip lock bag.

Fully-Loaded Chicken Salad

Yeah sure, chicken salad is usually quite Keto already. But taste this one, and you'll never need another recipe. It works perfectly as lunch you can pull out of your fridge all week, and it's also an awesome dinner option for those days when you just can't be bothered cooking.

Serves: 4
Time: 20 mins
- Calories: 561
- Net carbs: 2g
- Protein: 61g
- Fat: 35g

Ingredients:
- 1 boneless chicken breast
- 1 Tbsp. extra virgin olive oil
- ¼ tsp. salt
- ¼ tsp. black pepper
- 1 avocado, diced
- 4 oz. mozzarella balls
- 1 large tomato, diced
- 1 jar artichoke hearts
- ½ red onion, sliced
- 5 asparagus
- 20 leaves basil
- 4 cups baby spinach

For the dressing...
- 2 Tbsp. extra virgin olive oil
- 1 ½ Tbsp. balsamic vinegar
- 1 tsp. Dijon mustard
- 1 clove garlic
- Pinch salt and pepper

Method:
1. Take the chicken breast and slice in half lengthwise, then season well.
2. Add the olive oil to a skillet, place over a medium heat and cook for 3 minutes on each side until brown and cooked through.
3. Next add the asparagus and cook for a few more minutes.
4. Remove the chicken and slice well. Cool.

5. Take a small bowl and add the garlic, olive oil, vinegar, mustard and salt and pepper. Stir well to make the dressing.
6. Next place the baby spinach in a bowl, add the remaining ingredients and stir well.
7. Pop into serving containers and store until needed.

Sesame Salmon with Baby Bok Choy & Mushrooms

Salmon is a fast and easy option for lunchtimes. I love to inject this into my meal plans at least once or twice per month because it's so darn good. Besides, it boasts a whole load of healthy fats, minerals and antioxidants, it's quick to make and when it's marinates like this, tastes amazing...

Serves: 4

Time: 30 mins (plus 1-hour marinating time)

- Calories: 146
- Net carbs: 5g
- Protein: 10g
- Fat: 9g

Ingredients:

For the salmon...

- 4 x 4- 6 oz. salmon fillet
- 2 Portobello mushroom caps
- 4 baby Bok Choy
- 1 Tbsp. sesame seeds, toasted
- Green onions, to taste

For the marinade...

- 1 Tbsp. olive oil
- 1 tsp. sesame oil
- 1 Tbsp. coconut aminos
- ½ inch ginger, grated
- ½ tsp. lemon juice
- ½ tsp. salt
- ½ tsp. black pepper

Method:

1. Grab a small bowl and combine all the marinade ingredients.
2. Next place the salmon onto a large plate and pour over half the marinade. Pop into the fridge for an hour for the flavors to work their magic.
3. Preheat the oven to 400°F and grease and line a baking tray.
4. Prepare your veggies, pop into a large bowl and over with the remaining marinade. Stir well to combine then pop onto a baking tray.
5. Place the salmon onto the baking tray, skin down.
6. Pop into the oven and cook for 20 minutes.
7. Remove from the oven and allow to cool.
8. Divide into storage containers and cover with the sliced onions and sesame seeds.

Almond Butter Bacon Burger

Everyone loves bacon burgers for lunch, don't they? Well, I guess you've never tried bacon burgers like these. Drizzled with almond butter sauce, and dazzled with flavor, they'll make you feel like you've died and gone to Thailand. Or heaven. Or both.

Serves: 4

Time: 30 mins

- Calories: 890
- Net carbs: 8g
- Protein: 54.4g
- Fat: 68g

Ingredients:

For the almond butter sauce...

- 1 cup almond butter
- 1 cup water
- 4 garlic cloves, peeled
- 4 fresh Thai chili peppers
- 6 Tbsp. coconut amino
- 1 tsp. sweetener
- 1 Tbsp. rice vinegar

For the burger...

- 1 ½ lb. ground beef
- 4 slices Pepper Jack cheese
- 8 slices uncured bacon
- 1 large red onion
- 8 large leaves romaine lettuce
- Salt and pepper, to taste

Method:

1. Start by making the sauce. Place the almond butter and water into a small pan, place over a low heat and simmer until thick.
2. Add the coconut aminos and mix.
3. Place the garlic, chili, vinegar, and Swerve into a blender and pop into the almond butter sauce. Stir well.
4. Remove from the heat and pop to one side.
5. Then let's turn our attention to the burgers.
6. Place the ground beef into a bowl and shape into four. Make a thumbprint in the middle of each, sprinkle with salt and pepper, then pop under a broiler.
7. Cook until golden brown, turning often.

8. Place the cheese sliced over the top and return to the oven for a further 5 mins.
9. Meanwhile, fry the bacon and drain.
10. Allow to cool then pop everything into zip lock bags and store until needed.
11. When it's time to serve, assemble by placing the lettuce on the bottom, followed by the patties, some of the sauce and then the bacon.

Shrimp Avocado Salad with Tomatoes and Feta

This shrimp salad is so fast, AND it retains all the flavors for so many days that you might want to add it to your go-to list. It reminds me of Mediterranean holidays with my partner, wide open sea views, lemon juice and sunshine.

Serves: 2

Time: 20 mins

- Calories: 430
- Net carbs: 6.5g
- Protein: 24g
- Fat: 33g

Ingredients:

- 8 oz. shrimp
- 1 large avocado
- 1 small beefsteak tomato
- 1/3 cup crumbled feta cheese
- 1/3 cup freshly chopped cilantro or parsley
- 2 Tbsp. salted butter
- 1 Tbsp. lemon juice
- 1 Tbsp. olive oil
- ¼ tsp. salt
- ¼ tsp. black pepper

Method:

1. Place the shrimp into a bowl and add the melted butter. Stir well until coated.
2. Pop a skillet over a medium heat and add the shrimp. Cook for a minute or two on each side and pop onto a plate. Leave to cool.
3. Meanwhile, grab a large bowl and add the remaining ingredients. Stir well.
4. Add the shrimp and stir again.
5. Divide into storage containers and pop into the fridge until needed.

Thai Chicken Noodle Soup

I'll admit that I was more than a bit dubious about those zoodles before I'd ever tasted them. I mean…how could something make of vegetables ever be a patch on my favorite noodles. This utterly amazing soup soon changed my mind. It has all the best bits of Thai food- the curry paste, the coconut, the spice. You'll love it too. Trust me.

Serves: 8-9

Time: 30 mins

- Calories: 271
- Net carbs: 8.9g
- Protein: 24.4g
- Fat: 14.9g

Ingredients:

- 1 Tbsp. coconut oil
- ½ onion, chopped
- 1 jalapeño
- 1 ½ Tbsp. green curry paste
- 2 cloves garlic, minced
- 6 cups chicken bone broth
- 1 x 15 oz. can coconut milk
- 1 red pepper
- 1 lb. chicken breasts or thighs
- 2 Tbsp. fish sauce
- ½ cup chopped cilantro
- 2 medium zucchinis, cut into zoodles
- 1 lime, cut into 8 wedges

Method:

1. Melt the coconut oil in a pan then add the onions and cook until soft.
2. Stir through the jalapeño, curry paste and garlic and cook for another minute.
3. Pour in the broth and coconut milk and bring to the boil.
4. Reduce the heat and add the remaining ingredients, except the cilantro and zucchini.
5. Simmer until the chicken is cooked through.
6. Cool and stir through the cilantro.
7. Divide into storage containers, keeping the zoodles separate until serving day.
8. Serve zoodles with the soup ladled over the top and with a squeeze of lime.

Lasagna Stuffed Portobellos

These delicious stuffed mushrooms make an awesome alternative lunch when you're pressed for ideas and chicken salad just won't do it for you anymore. Pile up the cheese, throw it all in the oven and you're good to go!

Serves: 4

Time: 1-hour approx.

- Calories: 482
- Net carbs: 6.5g
- Protein: 28g
- Fat: 36g

Ingredients:

- 4 large portobello mushrooms, cleaned and dried
- 4 links Italian sausage
- 1 cup whole milk ricotta cheese
- 1 cup marinara sauce (recipe available in this book)
- 1 cup mozzarella cheese, shredded
- Chopped parsley to garnish if desired

Method:

1. First grease a baking tray and preheat your oven to 375°F.
2. Use a spoon to scrape out the brown part of the mushrooms then pop to one side.
3. Slice open the sausage and remove the meat from inside.
4. With your hands, form the meat into four patties. Press one into each mushroom cap, making sure to fill the whole space.
5. Top the patties with the ricotta, followed by the marinara sauce and the mozzarella.
6. Sprinkle cheese over the top then pop onto the baking tray.
7. Place into the oven and bake for 40 minutes until the cheese has melted.
8. Remove from the oven and allow to cool.
9. Pop into storage bags and store until needed.
10. These babies taste best when reheated.

Marinated Cauliflower Antipasto Salad

This recipe came my way via an Italian friend who invited me over for dinner one night. I'd warned him I was following Keto, but he reassured me he had the perfect dish, and this is the result. It makes a gorgeous, filling lunch (which is sure to impress) but also works well as part of a bigger meal, or even Keto tapas. Now there's a thought....

Serves: 6

Time: 10 mins (plus 6 hours marinating time)

- Calories: 216
- Net carbs: 8g
- Protein: 8g
- Fat: 13g

Ingredients:

- 1 medium head cauliflower, cut into bite sized pieces
- 1 cup marinated mushrooms, sliced
- 2 oz. salami, cut into strips
- 2 oz. Provolone cheese, cut into strips
- 1 x 6 oz. can black olives, drained and cut in half
- 1 x 12 oz. jar roasted red peppers, drained and cut into strips
- 3 Tbsp. capers, drained

For the dressing...

- ¼ cup vinaigrette dressing (check it's low sugar)
- 1 Tbsp. olive oil
- 2 Tbsp. freshly-squeezed lemon juice
- 1 Tbsp. juice from the jar of capers
- ½ tsp. dried Greek oregano

Method:

1. Start by steaming the cauliflower until tender. This should take around 4 minutes.
2. Remove and drain in a colander.
3. Meanwhile grab a small bowl and add the vinaigrette, olive oil, lemon juice, caper juice and oregano. Whisk well to combine.
4. Use a clean tea towel to dry the cauliflower then place into a large bowl.
5. Add half the dressing, stir well and pop into the fridge to marinate for around 6 hours (or overnight if you can).
6. Remove from the fridge and add the salami, Provolone, red peppers, mushrooms, olives and capers. Stir well to combine.
7. Season with salt and pepper, then stir again.
8. Divide into storage containers and pop into the fridge until needed.

Italian Chicken Bowls

What do you get if you take chicken, an abundance of herbs, a generous helping of fresh tomatoes AND plenty of garlic?

These Italian chicken bowls, that's what! They're similar to Buddha bowls in that you get your 'grain', protein and veggies in one bowl which you can adorn with extra toppings or whatever your heart desires. Try it!

Serves: 4

Time: 30 mins

- Calories: 305
- Net carbs: 5g
- Protein: 53g
- Fat: 6.4g

Ingredients:

- 1 tsp. salt
- ½ tsp. pepper
- 2 tsp. basil
- 2 tsp. marjoram
- 2 tsp. rosemary
- 2 tsp. thyme
- 1 tsp. paprika
- 2 lb. boneless skinless chicken breasts, cut into bite sized pieces
- 1 ½ cup broccoli florets
- 1 small red onion, chopped
- 1 cup plum tomatoes
- 1 medium zucchini, chopped
- 2 tsp. garlic minced
- 2 Tbsp. olive oil
- 2-4 cups cauliflower rice (optional)

Method:

1. First line a baking dish with foil and preheat your oven to 450°F.
2. Grab a small bowl and combine the salt, pepper, basil, marjoram, rosemary, thyme and paprika. Stir well.
3. Pop the chicken and vegetables into the baking dish (but not the cauliflower rice), add the herb mixture and olive oil, then give it a good stir.
4. Pop into the oven for 15-20 minutes until everything is cooked nicely.
5. Remove from the oven and allow to cool.

6. Place the cauliflower rice into each of your storage containers, followed by the chicken and veggie mixture.
7. Store until needed.

Thai Tuna Salad

This tuna salad is sooo quick and easy to prepare, blink and you'll miss it! That means there are no excuses- you HAVE TO make this part of your regular meal prep for the week. Yum!

Serves: 4
Time: 10 mins

- Calories: 524
- Net carbs: 7g
- Protein: 46g
- Fat: 33g

Ingredients:

- 3 x 70g cans tuna, drained
- 1 medium red bell pepper, diced
- ½ red onion, diced
- 1 cucumber, sliced thinly and diced
- ¼ cup sesame oil
- Juice of 1 lime
- Salt and pepper, to taste
- Sesame seeds, as garnish

Method:

1. Grab a large bowl and add the tuna. Use a fork to flake the fish well.
2. Next add the remaining ingredients (except the sesame seeds) and stir well to combine.
3. Pop into your storage containers, sprinkle with the sesame seeds and store until needed.

Broccoli & Cheese Soup

Broccoli soup could well be the best soup on the planet. Why? Because it gives your body all the nutrition it needs to get you on the top of your game, every mouthful is velvety, rich and gorgeous, the cheese flows over your taste buds, the nutmeg tweaks the edges and the parsley tops it all off with chlorophyll goodness. WOW!

Serves: 8
Time: 30 mins
- Calories: 291
- Net carbs: 4g
- Protein: 13g
- Fat: 25g

Ingredients:
For the soup...
- 2 Tbsp. butter
- ¼ onion, diced
- 2 garlic cloves minced
- 4 cups chicken broth
- 1 cup heavy whipping cream
- 14 oz. frozen broccoli florets or 4 cups fresh
- 3 cups cheddar cheese
- 3 slices Swiss cheese
- 1 oz. cream cheese softened
- ¼ tsp. nutmeg
- 1 tsp. parsley
- ½ tsp. pink salt
- ½ tsp. black pepper
- ¾ tsp. Xanthan gum (to thickens)

For the topping...
- 3 pieces bacon crumbled
- ½ cup shredded cheese

Method:
1. Place 3 cups of the broth with the broccoli in a large pan, pop over a medium heat and cook until the broccoli is tender.
2. Meanwhile, pop the butter into a skillet and melt over a medium heat. Cook the onions and garlic for around 5 minutes until cooked through.
3. Add the remaining broth, cream, cream cheese, spices and seasonings and stir well.
4. Bring to a boil, whisking continuously.

5. Add the cheese and continue to stir as it melts, then reduce the heat and simmer for 5 minutes.
6. Pour the cheese sauce into the cooked broccoli, stir well and simmer for a further 5 minutes.
7. Remove from the heat, stir through the Xanthan gum if using and leave to cool.
8. Divide between storage containers and store until needed.

Caribbean Jerk Shrimp with Cauliflower Rice

Is it me, or can I hear the sound of steel drums in the distance and feel those light Caribbean breezes wafting over my skin? Oops it must just be my dinner. Try it and you'll see why it's made my mouth water.

You'll notice that there are a couple of less-than-Keto-friendly ingredients such as orange juice and kidney beans which you might want to replace or ditch completely. It's up to you. Your diet, your life.

Serves: 4
Time: 45 mins

- Calories: 324
- Net carbs: 36g
- Protein: 24g
- Fat: 12.6g

Ingredients:

- 10 oz. large shrimp, peeled and deveined
- 2 Tbsp. olive oil
- 2 Tbsp. red wine vinegar
- 2 Tbsp. fresh squeezed orange juice
- 1 Tbsp. sweetener
- 1 Tbsp. coconut aminos
- 2 Tbsp. green onions, chopped
- 1 Tbsp. jalapeño, seeded and finely chopped
- Lime wedges, if desired

For the Jerk seasoning…

- ½ tsp. garlic powder
- ¼ tsp. onion powder
- ¼ tsp. dried thyme
- ½ tsp. paprika
- 1/8 tsp. allspice
- 1/8 tsp. nutmeg
- ¼ tsp. cayenne pepper
- 1/8 tsp. sea salt

For the cauliflower rice…

- 1 Tbsp. olive oil
- 1 green bell pepper, chopped
- 1 jalapeño, seeded and finely chopped
- 1 cup fresh pineapple, chopped (opt.)

- 4 cups cauliflower rice
- 1 tsp. garlic powder
- ¼ tsp. sea salt
- ¼ tsp. pepper
- 1/8 tsp. cinnamon
- ¼ cup fresh squeezed orange juice (opt)
- 1 x 15 oz. can red kidney beans (opt)
- 2 Tbsp. cilantro, chopped

Method:
1. First take a medium bowl and add the jerk seasoning spices. Mix well and pop to one side.
2. Next take another bowl and add the olive oil, vinegar, orange juice, sweetener, soy, onions, jalapeno and seasoning. Stir well to combine.
3. Add the shrimp and marinate for about 30 minutes.
4. Make the cauliflower rice by sautéing the bell peppers, jalapeño and pineapple in the olive oil for 5 minutes, until tender.
5. Then add the cauliflower, garlic, seasoning, and orange juice (if using). Stir well and cook for another 5 minutes.
6. Add the kidney beans (if using), stir through and cook for another 2 minutes.
7. Remove from the heat, stir through the cilantro and allow to cool.
8. Pop the shrimp onto skewers and pop until the broiler for 5-10 minutes, turning often until cooked.
9. Meanwhile, place the reserved marinade into a small pan, pop over a medium heat and bring to the boil.
10. Reduce the heat and simmer for 10 minutes.
11. Allow everything to cool, then divide between storage containers and pop into the fridge until you're ready to enjoy!

Asian Chicken and Rainbow Veggies

I love the fact you can pretty much just throw this into your oven, and get on with the rest of your food prep. Then return just 40 minutes later and you'll have this colorful dish of awesomeness waiting for your attention. Amazing!

Serves: 4

Time: 40 mins

- Calories: 379
- Net carbs: 35g
- Protein: 31g
- Fat: 14g

Ingredients:

- 1 lb. boneless, skinless chicken breasts
- 1 Tbsp. sesame oil
- 2 Tbsp. soy sauce
- 2 Tbsp. sweetener
- 2 red bell peppers, diced
- 2 yellow bell peppers, diced
- 3 carrots, sliced
- ½ head broccoli, cut into florets
- 2 red onions, diced
- 2 Tbsp. extra-virgin olive oil
- Salt and pepper, to taste
- ¼ cup chopped fresh parsley, for serving

Method:

1. Grease a baking sheet and preheat your oven to 400°F.
2. Place the chicken onto the baking sheet and cover with the soy sauce and sesame oil. Cover well, using a small brush if needed.
3. Place the vegetables over the sheet, coat with veggies and season well.
4. Pop into the oven for 25-30 minutes until cooked through.
5. Remove from the oven, allow to cool and garnish with parsley.
6. Divide between storage containers until ready to be enjoyed!

Mushroom and Feta Casserole

Love mushrooms? Then you'll melt when you try this casserole. It tastes incredible, it's easy to make and it makes several portions that will keep your stomach happy throughout the week. Brilliant!

Serves: 8

Time: 55 mins

- Calories: 181
- Net carbs: 5g
- Protein: 13g
- Fat: 13g

Ingredients:

- 12 free-range eggs
- 1 Tbsp. milk or cream
- 1 lb. mushrooms, washed and sliced
- 2 tsp. olive oil
- 1 cup crumbled Feta cheese
- 1/3 cup sliced green onions
- 1 tsp. seasoning of your choice
- Pepper, to taste

Method:

1. First preheat the oven to 375°C and grease a casserole dish.
2. Place the oil in a skillet, pop over a medium heat and add the mushrooms. Cook for 5 minutes, then place into the bottom of the casserole dish
3. Add the feta and onions.
4. Whisk the eggs together and pour over the veggies and cheese in the casserole dish.
5. Stir gently, season to your requirements then pop into the oven.
6. Bake for 30 minutes until the eggs are set and the top is browning nicely.
7. Remove from the oven and allow to cool completely before dividing into portions and storing.

Caesar Salad

Caesar salad is one of my all-time favorite salads. And this one is even better than the regular kind. (Yes, I know I say that all the time, but it's true!). Whizz up your own epic Keto mayo, mix with the usual lettuce leaves and top with pork rind to make something amazing. Mmm... my mouth is watering just thinking of it now.

Serves: 4

Time: 15 mins

- Calories: 727
- Net carbs: 1.8g
- Protein: 13g
- Fat: 38.7g

Ingredients:

- 1 egg yolk
- 8 Tbsp. avocado oil
- 3 Tbsp. apple cider vinegar
- 1 tsp. Dijon mustard
- 4 anchovy filets
- 2 garlic cloves
- 4 Tbsp. grated parmesan
- 24 whole leaves of romaine hearts
- 2 oz. pork rinds, chopped in small pieces
- 4 Tbsp. shaved Parmesan for garnish

Method:

1. Grab your blender and add the egg yolk, vinegar, and mustard. Slowly add the avocado oil, then start the blender. This should slowly create mayonnaise. Yay!
2. Open the blender, add the anchovies, garlic and Parmesan and blend again.
3. Divide into storage containers with the romaine lettuce and pork rind (but not mixed) and pop into the fridge.
4. On serving day, mix it all together and enjoy!

Thai Coconut Soup with Shrimp or Chicken

Yes, I know this is the second Thai soup in this book, but I'm sure you'll agree that it's really something special. When you take the time to make a broth using real ingredients, you can't help but notice how epic the flavor is. It's just like you're there in Thailand, buying the street food. Make the effort- it's worth it.

Serves: 2

Time: 30 mins

- Calories: 493
- Net carbs: 8g
- Protein: 11.5g
- Fat: 45.3g

Ingredients:

For the broth...

- 4 cups chicken broth
- 1 ½ cups full fat coconut milk
- 3 Kaffir lime leaves (or zest of a lime)
- 1-inch fresh lemongrass cut in slices (or 1 tsp. dried lemongrass)
- 1 cup fresh cilantro
- 3 or 4 dried Thai chilies (or 1 jalapeno sliced)
- 1-inch piece fresh ginger root
- 1 tsp. salt

For the soup...

- 4 oz. raw wild caught shrimp (or 4 oz. raw chicken thigh meat)
- 1 Tbsp. coconut oil
- 1 ½ oz. mushrooms, sliced
- 1 ½ oz. red onion, sliced thinly
- 1 Tbsp. fish sauce
- Juice of 1 lime
- 1 Tbsp. chopped cilantro, to garnish

Method:

1. Start by putting all the broth ingredients into a pan, pop over a medium heat and allow to simmer.
2. Cook for 20 minutes then strain and pour back into your pan.
3. Pop back over the heat and add the shrimp or chicken, fish sauce, onion and mushrooms.
4. Simmer for 10 minutes, until the meat is cooked.
5. Remove from the heat and stir through the line juice.
6. Pop into storage containers, sprinkle with the coriander and store until needed.

Lime Chicken Chowder

This lime chicken is creamy, tasty, garlicky and it definitely has that mouth-feel that leaves you feeling satisfied. I love the way the flavors continue to blend after cooking, and you'll find that your prepped meals taste even better with each bite.

Serves: 2-3

Time: 50 mins

- Calories: 519
- Net carbs: 8g
- Protein: 38g
- Fat: 34g

Ingredients:

- 1 lb. chicken thighs, boneless and skinless
- 8 oz. cream cheese
- 1 cup chicken broth
- 1 can diced tomatoes
- 1 small onion, diced
- 1 jalapeno, diced
- 1 lime, juiced
- 2 Tbsp. cilantro, chopped (optional)
- 1 clove garlic, chopped
- Liquid smoke, to taste (optional)
- 1 tsp. salt
- 1 Tbsp. pepper

To serve...

- Shredded cheese
- Lime wedge
- Chopped fresh cilantro

Method:

1. Grease a casserole dish and preheat the oven to 400°F.
2. Place all the ingredients into the casserole dish and stir well to combine.
3. Pop into the oven and cook for 45 minutes until the meat has cooked through.
4. Check that the meat has cooked, and if not, return it to the oven.
5. Remove from the oven when finally cooked and leave to cool.
6. Divide between storage containers, add the cheese, lime and cilantro and store until needed.

Pork Egg Roll in a Bowl

Pork + ginger + veggies can equal nothing less than WOW. Again, it's fast, it's yummy and you can have it meal prepped and away in the fridge in the blink of an eye!

Serves: 4
Time: 25 mins

- Calories: 255
- Net carbs: 4.2g
- Protein: 15g
- Fat: 18g

Ingredients:

- 2 Tbsp. sesame oil
- 3 cloves garlic, minced
- ½ cup onion, diced
- 5 green onions, sliced (white and green parts)
- 1 lb. ground pork
- ½ tsp. ground ginger
- Salt and black pepper, to taste
- 1 Tbsp. Sriracha
- 14 oz. bag coleslaw mix
- 3 Tbsp. coconut aminos
- 1 Tbsp. rice vinegar
- 2 Tbsp. toasted sesame seeds

Method:

1. Start by popping the sesame oil in a skillet and placing over a medium heat.
2. Add the onion, garlic and white part of the green onions. Cook for five minutes.
3. Next add the pork, ginger, salt, pepper and Sriracha. Cook through.
4. Finally, add the coleslaw mix, coconut aminos and vinegar. Cook until the veggies are soft.
5. Remove from the heat then cool completely.
6. Pop into storage containers, top with green onions and sesame seeds, and store until needed.

Vietnamese Banh Mi Meatballs

If you love Chinese buffet, you'll adore these amazing meatballs. I've tried to keep the ingredients as authentic as possible, but you can switch it up a bit using a regular radish and regular chili sauce if you like.

Serves: 4

Time: 30 mins (plus 1-hour marinating time)

- Calories: 529
- Net carbs: 6g
- Protein: 25g
- Fat: 45g

Ingredients:

For the pickled vegetables...

- 1 medium daikon radish, spiralized or julienne cut
- 1 medium carrot, spiralized or julienne cut
- 1/3 cup unseasoned (no sugar added) rice wine vinegar
- ¼ cup granulated sugar substitute
- 1 tsp. fish sauce

For the meatballs...

- 1 lb. ground pork
- 1 free-range egg
- ¼ cup almond flour
- 1 tsp. minced ginger
- ¼ cup scallions, chopped
- 2 Tbsp. fresh cilantro, chopped
- 2 Tbsp. fish sauce
- 1 Tbsp. sweetener
- ¼ tsp. salt
- ½ tsp. garlic powder

For the mayonnaise...

- ½ cup mayonnaise
- 1 Tbsp. Sriracha hot sauce
- 1 Tbsp. granulated sugar substitute
- 1 tsp. rice wine vinegar

For the garnish...

- ¼ cup sliced scallions
- ¼ cup chopped cilantro

Method:

1. Make the pickled veggies first by placing the daikon and carrot into a medium bowl.
2. Take another bowl and combine the vinegar, fish sauce and sweetener. Pop into the fridge for one hour.
3. Now let's make the meatballs. Place all ingredients into a medium bowl and mix, then divide into 16 balls.
4. Warm some oil in a skillet and cook the meatballs over a medium heat until brown. Pop to one side to cool.
5. Finally, make the mayonnaise by popping all ingredients into a bowl and stirring well.
6. Divide the meatballs between the storage containers, add the pickled veggies and a good dollop of the mayo.
7. Top with fresh cilantro and green onions, then store until needed.

Keto Bacon Sausage Meatballs

This Italian sausage recipe isn't just easy. It's also super nutritious, naturally protein-rich and it will lift the dullest of lunchtimes to epic new levels. If you're a bit fan (like me!) then you can nibble them for a snack, at dinner time, or whenever your heart desires. Yum!

Serves: 9

Time: 30 mins

- Calories: 630
- Net carbs: 2g
- Protein: 12g
- Fat: 7g

Ingredients:

- 1 lb. spicy Italian sausage
- Oil, for greasing
- 9 rashers bacon
- 2 Tbsp. garlic, minced
- 2 Tbsp. onion, diced
- 1 Tbsp. dried oregano

Method:

1. Grease a muffin tin with oil and preheat your oven to 375°F.
2. Now take a large mixing bowl and combine the sausage, garlic, onion and oregano. Stir well to combine.
3. Form into nine balls, then wrap each with a slice of bacon and place into the muffin tin.
4. Pop into the oven and bake for 30 minutes.
5. Remove from the oven and allow to cool completely.
6. Place into storage containers and store until needed.

Cream Cheese & Salami Pinwheels

I love how easy this recipe is! It's amazing. And you get plenty of protein and healthy fats with a ton of taste too.

Serves: 4
Time: 15 mins

- Calories: 47
- Net carbs: 0.8g
- Protein: 1g
- Fat: 4.2g

Ingredients:

- 4 x 8 oz. block cream cheese, at room temperature
- 32-40 thin slices pepperoni and genoa salami
- 1 lb. finely diced pickles

Method:

1. Place a large piece of plastic wrap over your counter.
2. Whip the cream cheese until flurry then spread ¼ of it into the center of the plastic wrap, making a ¼ inch thick rectangle.
3. Cover with the pickles, then the salami, until everything is covered.
4. Using another piece of plastic wrap, gently press everything down and then flip over so the cream cheese side is on top. Peel off the plastic.
5. Now roll up, removing the plastic layer at the bottom gently.
6. Wrap tightly in more plastic and pop into the fridge.
7. Repeat with the remaining ingredients then store everything in the fridge.
8. Slice and enjoy whenever you like.

Cheeseburger Lettuce Wraps

Yep, you can still have cheeseburgers on Keto. But not the fatty version which has been stuffed into a high-carb bun. Instead, wrap it lovingly in lettuce, pimp with whatever topping your love and you'll have an awesome meal-prep worthy lunch.

Serves: 6

Time: 20 mins

- Calories: 684
- Net carbs: 5g
- Protein: 48g
- Fat: 51g

Ingredients:

- 2 lb. ground beef
- ½ tsp. seasoned salt
- 1 tsp. black pepper
- 1 tsp. dried oregano
- 6 slices American cheese
- 2 large heads iceberg lettuce
- 2 tomatoes, sliced thin
- Small red onion, sliced thin

Method:

1. Grab a large bowl and add the beef, salt, pepper and oregano. Stir well to combine.
2. Divide the mixture into six balls then flatten into a burger shape.
3. Pop some oil into a skillet and place over a medium heat. Cook the burgers for 5 minutes on each side until cooked.
4. Remove from the heat and cool.
5. Pop into storage containers with the salad and cheese, then pop into the fridge.
6. Serve and enjoy when needed.

Chicken Enchilada Bowl

What I love most about these chicken enchiladas is the fact that you can whip them up and throw on pretty much whatever toppings you want. Hell- if you want to pack your storage containers with a different side salad for every day, then go for it!

Serves: 4
Time: 30 mins

- Calories: 120
- Net carbs: 5g
- Protein: 18g
- Fat: 2g

Ingredients:

- 1 lb. chicken breasts
- ¾ cups red enchilada sauce (sugar-free)
- ¼ cup water
- ¼ cup onion
- 1 x 4 oz. can green chilis
- 1 x 12 oz. steam bag cauliflower rice
- 1 Tbsp. olive oil

To garnish...

- Avocado
- Jalapeno
- Cheese
- Roma tomatoes
- Seasoning, to taste
- Other toppings of your choice

Method:

1. Place the oil in a skillet and pop over a medium heat. Cook the chicken breasts until brown.
2. Next add the sauce, chilis, onions and water, stir well then cover.
3. Reduce the heat to a simmer and cook until the chicken is just how you like it.
4. Remove the chicken from the pan, shred using two forks then return to the pan.
5. Cook for an extra 10 minutes until the sauce thickens.
6. Remove from the heat and allow to cool.
7. Prepare the cauliflower rice according to your taste and allow to cool.
8. Divide the cooled chicken into storage pots, add the cauliflower rice, cover with toppings and store until needed.

Flaxseed Keto Wraps

If you're still missing your flour tortillas or you're in bread detox, I highly recommend that you try these Flax wraps. It's super-easy to whip up a batch and store them for the week. Then just fill them with whatever salad and meat you desire, and you have an epic meal.

Serves: 4

Time: 5 mins

- Calories: 338
- Net carbs: 1.2g
- Protein: 11.6g
- Fat: 26.6g

Ingredients:

- 2 free-range eggs
- 6 Tbsp. flaxseeds, milled
- ¼ cup mozzarella, shredded
- 2 Tbsp. melted butter
- 3 Tbsp. water
- ½ tsp. baking powder
- Pinch of salt

Method:

1. Place all ingredients (except the butter) into a blender and hit that whizz button until smooth.
2. Pop the butter into a non-stick pan and pop over a medium heat.
3. Place a small spoonful of batter into the pan and swirl to form a pancake shape.
4. Flip, cook on both sides then pop to one side. Repeat with the remaining batter.
5. Pop into a storage container and keep until needed.

Italian Sub Roll-Ups

If you think you've tasted the best in Italian food, get ready to have your mind blown! These sub roll-ups are perfect for a protein-packed lunch, will fuel you through the rest of your afternoon and are so delicious, they might not make it to the storage boxes.

Serves: 4

Time: 5 mins

- Calories: 234
- Net carbs: 0.9g
- Protein: 10g
- Fat: 20.6g

Ingredients:

- 4 slices Genoa salami
- 4 slices Mortadella
- 4 slices Sopressata
- 4 slices Pepperoni
- 4 Slices Provolone
- Mayonnaise, to taste

To serve...

- Shredded lettuce
- Avocado oil or Olive oil
- Apple Cider vinegar
- Italian seasoning
- Toothpicks

Method:

1. Grab the largest slice of meat and lay it on your food prep surface.
2. Place the next largest slice on meat halfway on top, overlapping nicely.
3. Repeat with the rest of the meat slices.
4. Next spread some mayo on top, followed by the provolone and a small handful of lettuce, if using plus any extra toppings.
5. Roll up carefully and secure with a toothpick.
6. Repeat with the remaining ingredients and store carefully in plastic wrap, then pop into the fridge.
7. When you've done this, make a dip using 2:1 ratio of oil to vinegar, plus some herbs and seasonings. Pop into a storage container and place into the fridge.

Chicken Tenders

Got kids? Make this meal for them. They're the perfect finger food with an epic level of crunch that will keep them coming back for more. If you have a crowd to feel, double or even quadruple the batch and keep everyone happy all week.

Serves: 6

Time: 15 mins

- Calories: 285
- Net carbs: 3g
- Protein: 29.3g
- Fat: 14.7g

Ingredients:

- 8 oz. chicken breast tenderloins
- 1 cup almond flour
- 1 tsp. salt
- 1 tsp. pepper
- ¼ cup heavy whipping cream
- 1 large egg
- Olive oil, for frying

Method:

1. Grab a large bowl and add the egg and cream. Whisk together until smooth, add a pinch of salt and pepper, and whisk again.
2. Prepare the chicken and pop into the batter for about 10-15 minutes.
3. Meanwhile, place the almond flour onto a plate and season with salt and pepper.
4. Remove the chicken from the batter, allow the excess to drip away, then coat both sides of the chicken pieces in the almond flour mixture. Repeat with the rest of the mixture.
5. Place some olive oil into a non-stick pan and cook the chicken pieces on both sides until cooked through.
6. Pop to one side and allow to cool completely.
7. Place into storage containers and pop into the fridge until needed.

*Note: you can also part-cook the chicken pieces and store in the freezer if preferred.

Avocado Egg Salad (No Mayo)

You remember those Flax wraps I just told you about? You should definitely consider adding some of this stuff to them! Plenty of protein and healthy fats, plus a really well-rounded flavor will have them appearing on your meal prep list every week. Just be careful not to eat it all before you get it stored away safely.

Serves: 2

Time: 10 mins

- Calories: 199
- Net carbs: 2g
- Protein: 10g
- Fat: 15g

Ingredients:

- ½ large avocado
- 3 hard-boiled eggs, chopped
- 1 tsp. Dijon mustard
- 1 Tbsp. apple cider vinegar
- ¼ tsp. garlic powder
- ¼ tsp. dill weed
- ¼ tsp. salt
- 1 Tbsp. flat-leaf parsley, chopped

Method:

1. Grab a plate or a bowl and mash the avocado until smooth and creamy.
2. Throw in the rest of the ingredients and mix well.
3. Pop into a storage container and place into the fridge until needed.

Keto Poke with Ahi Tuna and Citrus

The first time I tried nuts with fish, I melted in my seat. It was THAT good. But the trouble is, peanuts aren't really allowed with Keto.

Luckily, we have a South East Asian store near my house which stocks every Keto-fan's favorite substitute- pili nuts. They're a low carb alternative to most nuts and they taste wonderful. (Of course, they do still contain carbs, so feel free to skip them if you're strict about Keto).

Cooks: 15 mins

Serves: 2

- Calories: 445
- Net carbs: 8g
- Protein: 39g
- Fat: 33g

Ingredients:

- 8 oz. Yellow Fin tuna (Ahi) fillet
- 1 Tbsp. coconut aminos
- ¼ cup chopped cilantro
- ½ Hass avocado
- 2 Tbsp. sesame oil
- 1 Tbsp. sesame seeds
- ¼ cup pili nuts
- 1 tsp. sea salt
- ¼ ruby red grapefruit

Method:

1. Place the fish into a large bowl and cover with the coconut aminos, sesame oil and salt. Stir gently to combine the flavors.
2. Add the remaining ingredients, stir well then season to taste.
3. Divide between serving containers and store until needed.

Bacon, Chicken & Tomato Stuffed Avocado

This is probably as easy as it gets. Make the filling, pack it with the avocado and stuff on serving day. Awesome!

Serves: 4
Time: 20 mins

- Calories: 341
- Net carbs: 5g
- Protein: 17g
- Fat: 28g

Ingredients:

- 2 chicken breasts, grilled
- 3 pieces bacon, cooked and chopped
- 2 avocados
- 1/3 cup grape tomatoes, chopped
- 1/3 cup mayonnaise
- Seasonings, to taste

Method:

1. Place the chicken into a medium bowl and sprinkle over the seasoning. Stir well until coated.
2. Add the tomatoes, onions, bacon and mayonnaise. Stir well until combined.
3. Place half of an avocado into each storage box and pile on top the chicken mixture.
4. If you're serving in a few days, it might be better to store the chicken mixture in boxes and leave the avocados whole until you're ready to serve.

Avocado Tuna Salad

Unlike many of the other salads in this book so far, this one is light, refreshing yet it really satisfies your tum. It's awesome for those hungry days, those tired days and those days when you just want to grab your meal prep box and go.

Serves: 6

Time: 10 mins

- Calories: 304
- Net carbs: 4g
- Protein: 22g
- Fat: 20g

Ingredients:

- 15 oz. tuna in oil, drained and flaked (3 small cans)
- 1 English cucumber, sliced
- 2 large avocados, peeled, pitted & sliced
- 1 medium red onion, thinly sliced
- ¼ cup cilantro
- 2 Tbsp. lemon juice, freshly squeezed
- 2 Tbsp. extra virgin olive oil
- 1 tsp. sea salt, or to taste
- 1/8 tsp. black pepper

Method:

1. Place the cucumber, avocado, onion, tuna and cilantro into a large bowl.
2. Add the lemon, olive oil, salt and pepper. Stir well to combine.
3. Divide between storage boxes then store until needed.

Dinners

The Ultimate Low-Carb Stir-Fry

Stir fries make an awesome Keto meal prep option because you can pack in the flavor, get plenty of veggies and have a whole meal that keeps for days and days. This is my favorite recipe. It's simple, it tastes amazing and it all comes together fast. Yum!

Serves: 2

Time: 10 mins

- Calories: 532
- Net carbs: 9g
- Protein: 47g
- Fat: 32g

Ingredients:

- 1 Tbsp. avocado oil
- 1 lb. ground chicken
- 2-3 cloves crushed garlic
- 1 Tbsp. peeled and grated ginger
- 1 bag mixed salad
- ¼ cup soy sauce
- 4 sliced scallions
- 1 Tbsp. sesame seed oil

Method:

1. Place the avocado oil into a wok or large pan.
2. Add the chicken and cook over a medium heat.
3. Next throw in the ginger and garlic and stir through.
4. Add the veggies and soy sauce and stir fry until cooked.
5. Remove from the heat and allow to cool before dividing between storage boxes.
6. Sprinkle with the scallions and sesame oil, and store until needed.

Cauliflower Fried Rice

Welcome to the wonderful world of cauliflower fried rice. It's tender, packed with vitamin C, and is guaranteed to leave you feeling satisfied. The original recipe contains carrots and peas, which can be higher carb, so just leave these out if you're strictly following Keto.

Serves: 6

Time: 25 mins

- Calories: 11
- Net carbs: 5g
- Protein: 4g
- Fat: 8g

Ingredients:

- 2 Tbsp. sesame oil or olive oil, divided
- 2 free-range eggs, beaten
- ¼ cup diced onion
- 2 cloves garlic
- ½ cup peas (opt.)
- ½ cup carrots (opt.)
- 1 medium head cauliflower
- 3 scallions, green part only
- 3 Tbsp. soy sauce or Tamari
- 1 tsp. sesame seeds

Method:

1. Turn your cauliflower into rice by whizzing in the food processor.
2. Place 1 tablespoon of oil into a skillet and pop over a medium heat. Add the cauliflower.
3. Add the eggs and stir well, cooking for a minute or two. Remove from the heat and pop onto a plate.
4. Add the rest of the oil, followed by the onion and garlic and cook for 2 minutes
5. Next throw in the peas and carrot and cook for another couple of minutes.
6. Add the cauliflower back into the pan and cook for five more minutes.
7. Throw in the soy sauce, stir through then remove from the heat and allow to cool.
8. Divide between storage boxes and store until needed.

Spiralized Pad Thai Chicken

More awesome Thai food which packs an epic nutritional punch AND piles up the flavor. This one is perfect for a simple meal prep dinner with a difference. Enjoy!

Serves: 4-6

Time: 20 mins

- Calories: 215
- Net carbs: 9g
- Protein: 21g
- Fat: 7g

Ingredients:

- 1 Tbsp. olive or coconut oil
- 1 small yellow onion, diced
- 4 chicken breasts
- 4 zucchinis, spiralized or cut into matchsticks
- 1 package carrot matchsticks
- ½ red cabbage, thinly chopped
- 2-3 scallions, sliced
- ¼ cup chopped peanuts or pili nuts (opt.)
- 1/3 cup chopped cilantro

For the Pad Thai sauce...

- ¼ cup tamarind paste
- 1 Tbsp. low-sodium soy sauce or tamari
- 1 Tbsp. peanut butter
- 2 cloves garlic, minced
- 2 tsp. fish sauce
- 2 tsp. lime juice

Method:

1. Grab a medium bowl and combine the sauce ingredients. Stir well.
2. Pop the oil into a pan and place over a medium heat. Add the onions and cook for 5 minutes until softening.
3. Add the chicken and about ¾ of the sauce. Stir well until combine. Cook for 10 minutes until chicken is cooked through.
4. Remove from the heat and stir through the zucchini noodles and the remaining sauce.
5. Pop over the heat again for 30 seconds, then remove and allow to cool completely.
6. Divide between storage containers then pop into the fridge until needed.

Greek Chicken Meal Prep Bowls

How about some Greek chicken? Yeah, you know this one is going to be good! Plenty of Mediterranean veggies, awesome feta cheese and plenty of Greek herbs...You can't go wrong, can you?

Serves: 4
Time: 20 mins

- Calories: 309
- Net carbs: 7g
- Protein: 30g
- Fat: 17g

Ingredients:

- 3 chicken breasts, diced
- 1 red pepper, diced
- 1 yellow pepper, diced
- 1 zucchini, thickly sliced
- 1 red onion, thickly sliced
- 2 Tbsp. olive oil
- 2 Tbsp. lemon juice
- 4 cloves garlic minced
- 1 Tbsp. oregano
- 1 tsp. salt
- ½ tsp. pepper
- ¼ cup feta cheese, crumbled

Method:

1. Grease a baking sheet and preheat your oven to 400°F.
2. Place all the ingredients (apart from the feta cheese) onto the baking sheet, stir well then pop into the oven for 20-30 minutes, until cooked.
3. Remove and allow to cool.
4. Place into storage containers, top with the feta and store until needed.

Mediterranean Broccoli Salad

Broccoli salad is the most underestimated dish ever, in my option. It's very easy, packed with antioxidants and it works amazingly well when teamed with a meal prep meat dish. Versatile enough for any meal, you're guaranteed to fall in love with this meal.

Serves: 8

Time: 25 mins

- Calories: 182
- Net carbs: 9g
- Protein: 5.9g
- Fat: 12.4g

Ingredients:

For the salad...

- 5 cups broccoli
- ½ cup artichoke hearts, marinated in olive oil
- ½ cup sundried tomatoes in olive oil
- ½ cup pitted Kalamata olives
- 1/3 cup red onion
- ¼ cup roasted salted sunflower seeds

For the dressing...

- 2 cups plain Greek yogurt
- Zest of large lemon
- 4 ½ tsp. Monk fruit (opt.)
- 1 ¾ tsp. dried oregano
- 1 ½ tsp. fresh garlic
- 1 ½ tsp. dried ground basil
- 1 ½ tsp. dried ground thyme
- 1 tsp. sea salt
- Pepper, to taste
- 2 Tbsp. oil from the jar of sun-dried tomatoes

Method:

1. Take a large bowl and add the salad ingredients. Stir well to combine.
2. Then take a medium bowl and add the dressing ingredients. Stir this well too.
3. Pour the dressing over the veggies and stir well.
4. Divide between storage containers and pop into the fridge until needed.

Zucchini Enchiladas

I ADORE Mexican food, so I've made it my mission to create great Keto alternatives to all my favorite dishes. Like these zucchini enchiladas. They're perfectly spiced, incredibly satisfying and a meal prep dish you'll fall in love with. Just one work- be careful when using pre-made sauce as they often contain sugars. In fact, why not make your own?

Serves: 4

Time: 40 mins

- Calories: 436
- Net carbs: 10g
- Protein: 33g
- Fat: 44g

Ingredients:

- 1 Tbsp. extra-virgin olive oil
- 1 large onion, chopped
- 2 cloves garlic, minced
- 2 tsp. ground cumin
- 2 tsp. chili powder
- 3 cups shredded chicken
- 1 1/3 cups red enchilada sauce, divided
- 4 large zucchini, halved lengthwise
- 1 cup shredded Monterey Jack
- 1 cup shredded Cheddar
- Salt, to taste

To serve...

- Sour cream, for drizzling
- Fresh cilantro, for garnish

Method:

1. Start by greasing a casserole dish and preheating the oven to 350°F.
2. Now pop the oil into a skillet, place it over a medium heat and cook the onion for 5 minutes.
3. Add the garlic, cumin and chili and cook again for a minute or so.
4. Add the chicken and sauce and stir until well combined.
5. Then make thin, wide slices of zucchini and place three, overlapping to make a 'wrap'.
6. Add a spoonful of the chicken, roll and place into the casserole dish.
7. Repeat with the remaining ingredients.

8. Add the remaining sauce, sprinkle with both cheeses and pop into the oven for 20 minutes.
9. Remove from the oven, allow to cool completely then divide into storage containers.
10. Add sour cream and cilantro (you can leave this bit until serving day) and store until needed.

Sesame Chicken

For me, sesame chicken just reminds me of the summer! Crunchy, mineral-rich, high in protein and irresistible, it works amazingly well with a side salad and cauliflower rice. Yum!

Serves: 2
Time: 15 mins
- Calories: 520
- Net carbs: 4g
- Protein: 45g
- Fat: 36g

Ingredients:

For the coated chicken...
- 1 free-range egg
- 1 Tbsp. arrowroot powder
- 1 lb. chicken thighs, cut into bite sized pieces
- 1 Tbsp. toasted sesame seed oil
- Salt and pepper, to taste

For the sesame sauce...
- 2 Tbsp. soy sauce
- 1 Tbsp. toasted sesame seed oil
- 2 Tbsp. sweetener (or to taste)
- 1 Tbsp. vinegar
- 1 tsp. grated ginger (opt.)
- 1 clove garlic, minced
- 2 Tbsp. sesame seeds
- ¼ tsp. Xanthan gum

Method:
1. First make the batter by combining the egg and the arrowroot. Whisk well.
2. Dip the chicken into this batter and coat well.
3. Place the sesame seed oil into a pan, pop over a medium heat and cook the chicken for about 10 minutes.
4. Make the sauce by placing the sauce ingredients into a bowl and whisking well.
5. Once the chicken has cooked, add this sauce to the pan and stir. Cook for five minutes.
6. Remove from the heat and allow to cool completely.
7. Transfer to storage containers, add some cooked broccoli, sprinkle with sesame seeds and onion, then serve when needed.

Bacon Ranch Chicken Casserole

Ranch chicken? Ooooh I don't mind if I do! It's sooo cheesy and creamy, it boasts exactly the right amount of flavorings and it's ready in less than an hour- perfect for meal prep. Just make sure you cook plenty of this stuff- it's addictive!

Serves: 8

Time: 40 mins

- Calories: 498
- Net carbs: 4g
- Protein: 37g
- Fat: 36g

Ingredients:

- 1 ½ lb. cooked chicken, cubed
- 1 lb. fresh broccoli, steamed
- 1 Tbsp. minced onion
- 1 Tbsp. parsley
- ½ Tbsp. garlic powder
- ½ Tbsp. dill
- ½ tsp. salt
- ½ tsp. pepper
- ¼ cup + 2 Tbsp. bacon crumbles
- 8 oz. cream cheese softened
- 4 oz. sour cream
- 4 oz. mayonnaise
- 8 oz. shredded cheddar

Method:

1. Start by greasing a casserole dish and preheating your oven to 350°F.
2. Grab a large bowl and combine the cream cheese, sour cream, mayonnaise and spices. Stir well to combine.
3. Next add the chicken, broccoli, ¾ of the cheese and the bacon (but retain some bacon for sprinkling).
4. Stir well then pop into the casserole dish.
5. Sprinkle with the rest of the cheese and remaining bacon then pop into the oven.
6. Cook for 35 minutes.
7. Remove from the oven and allow to cool completely.

Sheet Pan Chicken Fajitas

This has to be the easiest fajita meal on the planet. Perfect for meal prep and wonderful with just about everything, you need to make this Mexican dish a regular part of your life. Enjoy!

Serves: 4
Time: 40 mins
- Calories: 296
- Net carbs: 11g
- Protein: 25g
- Fat: 15g

Ingredients:
- 1 ½ lb. chicken breast, boneless & skinless
- Olive oil, to taste
- 1 Tbsp. taco seasoning
- 3 bell peppers, sliced
- 1 onion, sliced
- Fresh limes, to taste

Method:
1. Start by preheating your oven to 400°F and greasing a baking sheet.
2. Cut the chicken into strips then throw into a bowl.
3. Coat with the taco seasoning, drizzle with the olive oil and stir well to combine.
4. Chop the peppers, throw into the bowl with the chicken and stir again.
5. Pop everything onto the baking sheet and pop into the oven for 20-30 minutes until cooked.
6. Remove from the oven and allow to cool completely before dividing into storage containers.
7. Add some cauliflower rice, pico, guacamole and plenty of chili flakes to make it even more amazing!

Loaded Cauliflower Bake

Cauliflower cheese, but not as you know it! Serve this stuff with anything your heart desires or throw in your favorite meat to make an outstanding meal prep dish you can pull from the fridge and enjoy!

Serves: 4

Time: 45 mins

- Calories: 498
- Net carbs: 4.1g
- Protein: 13.9g
- Fat: 45g

Ingredients:

- 1 large head cauliflower, cut into florets
- 2 Tbsp. butter
- 1 cup heavy cream
- 2 oz. cream cheese
- 1 ¼ cup shredded sharp cheddar cheese, separated
- Salt and pepper, to taste
- 6 slices bacon, cooked and crumbled
- ¼ cup chopped green onions

Method:

1. Start by greasing a casserole dish and preheating your oven to 350°F.
2. Bring a pan of water to the boil and cool the cauliflower for 2 minutes, then drain immediately.
3. Take a pan and add the butter, heavy cream, cream cheese, 1 cup cheese, salt and pepper and stir well until combined. Pop over a medium heat and melt, stirring often.
4. Place the cauliflower into the casserole dish, top with the cheese sauce, most of the bacon (reserve some for sprinkling), and most of the green onions (again, reserve some for sprinkling!). Stir well.
5. Top with more cheese, the remaining bacon and the remaining green onions.
6. Pop in the oven and cook for about 30 minutes until cooked.
7. Remove from the oven and allow to cool completely.
8. Divide between storage containers and store until needed.

Turkey Sausage Frittata

Unlike most people, I don't think that eggs are just for breakfast. Because when you've had a long hard day, they provide everything your body needs to hit the reset button and feel awesome again. Packed with B-vitamins that will help you deal with stress and keep functioning at a super high level, plus a ton of protein, you might have found your perfect meal prep dinner in this recipe.

Serves: 8

Time: 40 mins

- Calories: 240
- Net carbs: 5.5g
- Protein: 16.7g
- Fat: 16.7g

Ingredients:

- 12 oz. ground turkey breakfast sausage
- 2 bell peppers
- 12 free-range eggs
- 1 cup sour cream
- 1 tsp. salt
- 1 tsp. black pepper
- 2 tsp. butter
- 2 oz. shredded cheddar

Method:

1. Start by preheating the oven to 350°F.
2. Grab your blender and add the eggs, sour cream and salt and pepper. Whizz for 30 seconds then pop to one side.
3. Place a skillet over a medium heat and add the butter.
4. Add the peppers and cook for 5 minutes, until brown. Remove and pop to one side.
5. Add the turkey sausage to the pan and cook for 8-10 minutes, until cooked.
6. Press the meat into the bottom of the pan, add the peppers then top with the egg mixture.
7. Pop into the oven and bake for 30 minutes.
8. Remove and allow to cool completely before dividing between storage containers.
9. Store until needed.

Berbere Stuffed Peppers

If you're not a fan of spicy food, don't make this recipe. Or at least, substitute the Berbere for sweet paprika instead. Berbere is a spice mix found in Ethiopia and my goodness, it's HOT. To reduce the carbs even further, switch the carrot for squash, or omit altogether.

Serves: 5

Time: 1 hour

- Calories: 516
- Net carbs: 8.4g
- Protein: 35g
- Fat: 38.8g

Ingredients:

- 2 lb. ground beef
- 1 cup cauliflower rice
- 3 Tbsp. butter
- ½ onion
- 1 large carrot (opt.)
- 2 cloves garlic
- 2 tsp. smoked sea salt
- 2 tsp. Berbere (can use chili power instead)
- 5 large bell peppers
- Sour cream, to taste

Method:

1. Preheat your oven to 400°F and grease a casserole dish. Pop to one side.
2. Place a skillet over a medium heat, add the butter and throw in the veggies.
3. Cook for 8-10 minutes, stirring well until tender.
4. Add the beef, salt and Berbere, stir well.
5. Add the cauliflower rice and stir well.
6. Cut off the tops of your peppers, remove the core and seeds, then fill with the beef mixture.
7. Pop into the casserole dish, add a spoon of sour cream, season well then pop into the oven.
8. Cook for 30-45 minutes until the peppers are cooked through.
9. Remove from the oven and allow to cool completely.
10. Divide between storage containers then store until needed.

Creamy Mushroom Chicken

This recipe is so simple, you can't help but fall in love with it. It's very budget-friendly, excellent when you want a satisfyingly creamy meal dinner, and wonderful when you need to watch the food budget. Increase the quantities as needed.

Serves: 2

Time: 25 mins

- Calories: 334
- Net carbs: 3.2g
- Protein: 24.3g
- Fat: 27.3g

Ingredients:

- 2 chicken breasts
- 1 small onion
- 5 cremini mushrooms
- ½ tsp. salt
- ½ tsp. dried thyme
- 3 Tbsp. butter, unsalted
- 1/3 cup full fat canned coconut milk

Method:

1. Start by heating a skillet over a medium heat, adding some butter and then the mushrooms and onions. Sprinkle with salt and cook for 5 mins.
2. Tip the onions and mushrooms onto a plate then pop to one side.
3. Place the chicken on a plate, cover with salt and thyme and pop into the skillet with the remaining butter.
4. Cook for five minutes then flip over. Cook for a further five minutes.
5. Add the mushrooms and onions, then pour in the coconut milk. Cook for another 5 minutes.
6. Bring to a simmer and cook for five minutes.
7. Remove from the heat, leave to cool and then divide between storage containers. Store until needed.

Shrimp Stir Fry with Cauliflower Rice

Shrimp makes an excellent meal prep dish because they contain wonderful amounts of protein, magnesium and calcium, plus they're ready in the blink of an eye. Throw them into a mouth-watering dish like this stir fry and your taste buds will be in heaven!

Serves: 4

Time: 25 mins

- Calories: 357
- Net carbs: 9g
- Protein: 24.7g
- Fat: 24.8g

Ingredients:

- 1 lb. shrimp (peeled, tail on)
- 2-inch ginger root
- 4 stalks green onion
- 2 garlic cloves
- 4 baby Bella mushrooms
- 1-inch lemon rind
- 2 tsp. salt
- 3 Tbsp. bacon fat
- 12 oz. riced cauliflower
- 2 Tbsp. olive oil

Method:

1. Preheat the oven to 400°F and grease a baking sheet.
2. Place the cauliflower rice on the baking sheet, spread well, drizzle with the oil, season with the salt and then pop into the oven for 10 minutes.
3. Next place a skillet over a medium heat, add the bacon fat then the remaining ingredients except the shrimp, coconut aminos and salt. Cook for a few minutes until tender.
4. Add the remaining ingredients, stir well and cook for another 3-5 minutes.
5. Remove from the heat and allow to cool completely.
6. Divide between storage containers and store until needed.

Spicy Mustard Thyme Chicken & Coconut Roasted Brussels Sprouts

Brussels sprouts are amazing. Don't believe me? Then get preparing this dish! When you roast them, the sprouts lose much of the bitter taste and end up soft, melt-in-the-mouth and epically moreish. Teamed with spicy mustard chicken and you have the perfect easy meal prep match!

Serves: 2

Time: 25 mins

- Calories: 528
- Net carbs: 8g
- Protein: 16g
- Fat: 4g

Ingredients:

- 1 lb. Brussels sprouts, halved
- 2 medium boneless chicken breasts
- ¼ cup mustard powder
- 1 Tbsp. lemon juice
- 1 tsp. thyme
- Salt and pepper, to taste
- 1 Tbsp. coconut oil, melted

Method:

1. Preheat the oven to 350°F and line a couple of baking sheets with parchment paper and grease a casserole dish. Pop to one side.
2. Take a medium bowl and add the mustard, lemon juice, salt, pepper and thyme. Mix well to combine.
3. Place the chicken breasts into this mixture, coat well and pop into the fridge for at least 10 minutes to marinate.
4. Remove from the fridge and bring to room temperature.
5. Meanwhile, place the Brussels sprouts into a medium bowl, add the coconut oil and salt and pepper and stir well to combine.
6. Place the sprouts onto the prepared baking sheets and pop to one side.
7. Place the chicken into the casserole dish and pop into the oven for 10 minutes. Then add the Brussels sprouts and cook for a further 15 minutes.
8. Remove from the oven, allow to cool completely and divide between storage containers.
9. Serve when needed.

Keto Pizza Crust

Want pizza? Your wish is my command! Just top with cheese, tomato and whatever other toppings your heart desires and your Keto pizza dreams will come true.

Serves: 8

Time: 20 mins

- Calories: 110
- Net carbs: 2g
- Protein: 9g
- Fat: 7g

Ingredients:

- 1 ½ cup Mozzarella cheese, shredded
- 2 Tbsp. cream cheese, cut into cubes
- 2 free-range egg, beaten
- 1/3 cup coconut flour

For the toppings...

- Tomato sauce
- Shredded cheese
- Red onion
- Pepperoni
- Mozzarella
- Fresh herbs
- Olives

Method:

1. Preheat your oven to 425°F and line a baking sheet with parchment paper.
2. Take a large bowl and add the mozzarella and cream cheese. Stir well then pop into the microwave for a minute or so until melted. Stir again.
3. Add the beaten eggs and the flour, then mix with your hands. You want to keep mixing until you form a dough.
4. Press the dough onto the baking sheet and prick with a fork.
5. Pop into the oven for around 10 minutes until brown.
6. If precooking the entire pizzas, remove from the oven and top with toppings before returning to the oven for a further 10 minutes, until the cheese melts. (Watch carefully)
7. If you're topping closer to serving day, remove from the oven and allow to cool completely.
8. Store until needed.

Lemon Chicken with Asparagus

Whenever I'm planning a gathering of people, or I want to treat myself for the week ahead, I make sure I add this lemon chicken recipe to my meal prep list for the week. It's light, delicious and super-easy to make. Perfect on all counts!

Serves: 4

Time: 30 mins

- Calories: 298
- Net carbs: 11g
- Protein: 35g
- Fat: 11g

Ingredients:

- 4 chicken breasts boneless, skinless
- ¼ cup coconut flour
- 2 Tbsp. olive oil
- ¾ tsp. sea salt
- ½ tsp. ground black pepper
- 1 lb. asparagus stalks, halved and ends trimmed
- 2 cloves garlic, crushed
- 3 Tbsp. fresh lemon juice
- Zest of ½ lemon
- 1 Tbsp. Dijon mustard
- 1 cup chicken stock
- 1 Tbsp. parsley, chopped

Method:

1. Grab a shallow dish and add the flour, salt and pepper. Stir well.
2. Add the chicken and coat well in the flour mixture.
3. Place a skillet over a medium heat and add a tablespoon of the olive oil.
4. Add the chicken and cook on each side for five minutes.
5. Remove from the heat and pop to one side.
6. Place the rest of the oil into the skillet, pop back over the heat and add the asparagus.
7. Cook for a minute, then add the garlic, stir well and cook for another minute.
8. Take a small bowl and add the lemon, mustard, zest and chicken stock. Stir well.
9. Pour this mixture over the asparagus and bring to the boil.
10. Reduce to a simmer and leave to cook for five minutes until the asparagus is tender.
11. Stir through the parsley and the chicken and coat everything nicely.
12. Remove from the heat and allow to cool completely.
13. Divide between storage containers and store until needed.

Cheesesteak Stuffed Bell Peppers

These bell peppers make an incredible addition to anyone's meal prep menu. Spicy, creamy and satisfying, you simply can't go wrong with them. Of course, I like to add lashings of chili flakes too so that I can take the spice to a whole new level. Enjoy!

Serves: 4

Time: 30 mins

- Calories: 394
- Net carbs: 8g
- Protein: 42g
- Fat: 20g

Ingredients:

- 12 oz. strip steak (sirloin), cut in to strips
- 3 oz. mushrooms
- 3 oz. onions
- 1 tsp. oregano
- 3 Tbsp. olive oil
- 5 oz. cheddar
- 5 oz. bell pepper
- 4 oz. cream cheese spread
- 1 oz. jalapeño

For the salad...

- 2 Tbsp. olive oil
- 6 oz. lettuce
- 3 oz. cherry tomatoes

Method:

1. Preheat the oven to 350°F and grease a baking sheet with oil.
2. Slice the tops off the pepper, remove the core and the seeds then place onto a baking tray. Cook for 20 minutes.
3. Place a skillet over a medium heat, add the olive oil and cook the onion for 5 minutes.
4. Next add the steak, mushrooms and oregano. Stir well and cook until steak looks tender.
5. Place this steak mixture into the bell peppers, top with cream cheese and layer.
6. Top with jalapeños and cheddar cheese, and pop into the oven for a further 5 minutes until the cheese melted.
7. Remove from the oven and allow to cool before dividing into storage containers.
8. Add the salad to the storage container, then store until needed.

Keto Lasagna with Zucchini Noodles

In this amazing Keto lasagna, zucchini takes the place of pasta sheets. Is there nothing that this amazing vegetable CAN'T do? Make your own marinara sauce if you can, or otherwise choose a decent Keto-friendly option from the store. Feel free to pimp this recipe up with plenty of herbs, extra cheese and whatever else you fancy.

Serves: 4

Time: 45 mins

- Calories: 544
- Net carbs: 4g
- Protein: 34g
- Fat: 41g

Ingredients:

- 1 lb. ground beef
- 1 Tbsp. olive oil
- 1 cup marinara sauce (recipe available in this book)
- 1 large zucchini
- 10 oz. ricotta cheese
- 4 oz. Mozzarella cheese, shredded

Method:

1. First preheat the oven to 350°F and grease a casserole dish.
2. Peel the zucchini into strips, sprinkle with salt and leave for 15 minutes.
3. Meanwhile, place the olive oil into a pan, pop over a medium heat and cook the beef until brown.
4. Add the sauce and salt and pepper, stir well and remove from the heat.
5. Now it's time to get layering! Start with a small layer of meat, top with zucchini, and add the ricotta. Repeat until all the ingredients have been used.
6. Top with mozzarella, season with salt and pepper and cover with foil.
7. Pop into the oven for 30 minutes until cooked.
8. Remove from the oven, allow to cool completely and divide between storage containers.
9. Store until needed.

Buffalo Wings

Everybody loves buffalo wings, don't they? Especially when they come with a crunchy Parmesan and pork crust. You really need to try these babies to believe it. Enjoy!

Serves: 4

Cooks: 30 minutes

- Calories: 350
- Net carbs: 0.5g
- Protein: 40g
- Fat: 15g

Ingredients:

- 1 lb. boneless, skinless chicken breast
- 1 ½ cups crushed pork rinds
- ½ cup grated Parmesan cheese
- ½ tsp. garlic powder
- ¾ cup hot sauce
- 2 Tbsp. butter

Method:

1. Preheat your oven to 425°F and grease a baking sheet.
2. Place the pork, parmesan and garlic into your food processor and pulse until fine and combined.
3. Place the mixture onto a plate and place your chicken chunks on another plate.
4. Press the chicken into the parmesan mixture, making sure it's all well-coated.
5. Next pop the butter into a skillet and place over a medium heat.
6. Cook the chicken for 5 minutes on each side until browned.
7. Place onto the baking sheet.
8. Take a medium bowl and combine the hot sauce and butter and pour over the chicken.
9. Pop into the oven and cook for 30 minutes, checking often.
10. Remove from the heat and allow to cool completely.
11. Pop into storage containers and store until needed.

Snacks & Sides

Cheesy Bacon Stuffed Mini Peppers

These tiny stuffed peppers were inspired by my trips to Spain where I enjoyed them with just about any meal I could! Now I'm at home, I like to indulge in them whenever I can. They make an epic snack, an excellent side dish and, sure, you can even eat them for breakfast if you fancy it.

Serves: 12
Time: 30 mins
- Calories: 87
- Net carbs: 1g
- Protein: 2g
- Fat: 7g

Ingredients:
- 6 mini sweet peppers
- 4 oz. cream cheese
- 2 Tbsp. green onions
- 4 slices bacon
- ½ tsp. garlic powder
- ½ cup shredded cheddar cheese + extra for topping
- 1 tsp. Worcestershire sauce (recipe available in this book)
- Chopped cilantro for topping

Method:
1. Start by preheating the oven to 400°F and grease a baking sheet.
2. Grab a blender and add the cream cheese, onions, bacon, garlic powder, cheddar and Worcestershire sauce. Hit whizz until smooth.
3. Open up the peppers and fill with this mixture.
4. Place onto the baking sheet, sprinkle with pepper and extra cheese, then pop into the oven for 10-15 minutes until cooked.
5. Remove from the oven, allow to cool completely then pop into storage containers until needed.

Superfood Meatballs

These meatballs are nothing like your regular meatballs. They're epic! They're nutritious, they're tasty and they'll keep you glowing with heath from the inside. These are awesome as a snack at any time of the day. Make one of our Keto friendly sauces and you'll be dipping happily for days.

Serves: 10
Cooks: 50 mins

- Calories: 323
- Net carbs: 4.3g
- Protein: 31.8g
- Fat: 21g

Ingredients:

- 3 lb. ground beef
- 1 lb. pastured chicken livers
- 1 large shallot
- 4 medium carrots
- 3 garlic cloves
- 2 Tbsp. grass fed butter
- 1 tsp. dried oregano
- 2 Tbsp. coconut aminos (separated)
- 3 tsp. salt (separated)
- 2 tsp. black pepper
- 1 tablespoon dried thyme (dried)
- 1 Tbsp. garlic powder
- Olive oil

Method:

1. Preheat the oven to 425°F and grease a baking sheet.
2. Pop a skillet over a medium heat, add some olive oil and cook the shallots, onion and garlic until soft.
3. Next add the chicken livers, 1 teaspoon of the salt and the oregano. Cook until brown.
4. Add the coconut aminos, 1 tablespoon apple cider vinegar and cook until the livers are cooked through.
5. Remove from the heat and leave to cool.
6. Pop into a food processor and chop until it looks like ground beef.
7. Place into a bowl with the rest of the salt and seasoning. Stir well.
8. Shape into balls and pop onto the baking sheet.

9. Drizzle with oil and pop into the oven for 5 minutes. Then turn down the temperature to 350°F and cook for a further 20 minutes.
10. Remove from the oven and allow to cool completely before dividing them between storage boxes and storing until needed.

Steak Bites

Everyone loves steak, right? So instead of opting for hard boiled eggs for your Keto snacks, why not take a little extra time and create these beauties instead. Packed with protein, taste and that satisfaction factor, you'll probably finish the lot much faster than you thought. Enjoy!

Serves: 2
Time: 20 mins

- Calories: 489
- Net carbs: 1g
- Protein: 23g
- Fat: 44g

Ingredients:

- ½ cup soy sauce
- 1/3 cup olive oil (plus extra for frying)
- ¼ cup Worcestershire sauce (recipe available in this book)
- 1 tsp. minced garlic
- 2 tablespoons dried basil
- 1 Tbsp. dried parsley
- 1 tsp. black pepper
- 1 ½ lb. sirloin steak, cut in 1-inch pieces

Method:

1. Grab a large bowl and add all the ingredients. Stir well.
2. Cover and pop in the fridge for a minimum of one hour, ideally overnight.
3. Place a small amount of olive oil into a skillet and pop over a medium heat.
4. Remove the steak from the marinade and cook in the pan until browned.
5. Remove the pan from the heat and allow to cool completely.
6. Divide between storage containers and store until needed.

Lemon Cashew Cookies

I know...you can't believe that I'm actually including an awesome cookie recipe in this meal prep book, right? Thank me later. But first get cooking these amazing sweet treats.

Serves: 12

Cooks: 25 mins

- Calories: 140
- Net carbs: 4g
- Protein: 4g
- Fat: 9g

Ingredients:

- 1 cup cashew butter
- 2 free-range eggs
- Zest and juice of a lemon
- ½ tsp. vanilla extract
- ¼ tsp. powdered stevia
- ¼ tsp. baking soda

Method:

1. Preheat the oven to 350°F and grease a baking sheet.
2. Place all the ingredients into a large bowl and mix well.
3. Take small drops of the batter and place onto a baking sheet.
4. Pop into the oven and bake for 10-15 minutes.
5. Cool completely then divide between airtight containers until needed.

Peaches and Cream Fat Bombs

No Keto book would be complete without at least one fat bomb recipe. And this peaches and cream version will pleasantly surprise you. Try them, you'll see!

Serves: 24

Time: 5 mins (plus freezing time of 4 hours)

- Calories: 43
- Net carbs: 0.9g
- Protein: 0.5g
- Fat: 4.2g

Ingredients:

- 4 Tbsp. unsalted butter, softened
- 6 oz. cream cheese, softened
- 1 cup frozen peaches, slightly warmed
- 3 ½ Tbsp. sweetener, separated

Method:

1. Throw all the ingredients into your food processor and whizz until combined.
2. Pour into a freezer mold and pop in the freezer for at least 4 hours.
3. Store in the freezer until ready to enjoy!

Avocado Brownies

Ooooh I don't mind if I do! These avocado brownies are astonishingly good. So good, in fact that I have trouble restraining myself. I recommend that you store them away in portions as fast as you possibly can before they start disappearing. Wow!

Serves: 12

Time: 45 mins

- Calories: 158
- Net carbs: 3g
- Protein: 3.8g
- Fat: 14g

Ingredients:

Wet ingredients...

- 8 oz. avocado (approx. 2)
- ½ tsp. vanilla
- 4 Tbsp. cocoa powder
- 1 tsp. sweetener
- 3 Tbsp. refined coconut oil
- 2 free-range eggs
- 1 x 3 ½ oz. bar dark chocolate (high cocoa percentage, no added sugar)

Dry ingredients...

- 1 cup blanched almond flour
- ¼ tsp. baking soda
- 1 tsp. baking powder
- ¼ tsp. salt
- ¼ cup erythritol

Method:

1. Preheat the oven to 350°F and line a baking dish with parchment paper.
2. Grab your food processor and add the avocados. Then add the remaining wet ingredients, whizzing until smooth.
3. Take another bowl, add the dry ingredients and stir well together.
4. Next add the wet ingredients into the dry ingredients, stirring gently to combine.
5. Pour into the baking dish and pop into the oven for 35 mins.
6. Remove from the oven and allow to cool before slicing into 12 pieces and popping into storage containers.
7. Store until needed.

Taco Cups

These little cheesy taco cups are sooo cute, you won't resist giving them a try. Best of all, you'll have enough to last you all week, so you can get maximum Keto goodness with far less effort. Double win!

Serves: 14

Time: 20 mins

- Calories: 221
- Net carbs: 0.9g
- Protein: 14.2g
- Fat: 17.1g

Ingredients:

- 4 ½ Tbsp. butter, melted and cooled
- 1/3 cup coconut flour
- 1 oz. cream cheese, softened
- 4 free-range eggs
- ¼ tsp. salt
- ¼ tsp. baking powder
- ½ tsp. garlic powder
- 1 1/3 cup cheddar cheese, shredded

Method:

1. Preheat the oven to 400°F and grease a muffin pan.
2. Grab a large bowl and add the eggs, salt, butter, and cream cheese. Whisk together until combined.
3. Add the coconut flour, baking powder and spices and stir well until combined.
4. Spoon into the pre-prepared muffin tins and press a whole in the middle with your fingers.
5. Pop into the oven and cook for 8 minutes.
6. Remove from the oven, add some taco meat into the holes, top with cheese and return to the oven. Bake for a further 5 minutes.
7. Remove from the oven, allow to cool completely and pop into storage containers until needed.

Cheesy Cloud Biscuits

Yum! Who'd have thought that cloud biscuits would taste this good on Keto? The cheese flavors really shine through without being too overpowering, allow you to fill them with whatever you fancy. Of course, you can just eat them plain from the oven, but that wouldn't exactly be meal prep...

Serves: 4

Time: 20 mins

- Calories: 522
- Net carbs: 6g
- Protein: 30g
- Fat: 41g

Ingredients:

- 1 free-range egg
- ¾ cup cheddar cheese
- 1 Tbsp. heavy cream
- 4 oz. almond flour
- 1 tsp. baking powder
- 1 tsp. cayenne pepper

For the toppings...

- 8 oz. smoked salmon
- 4 oz. cream cheese spread
- 2 Tbsp. red onion
- Fresh dill (optional)
- Juice of one lemon
- Arugula (rocket)

Method:

1. Preheat the oven to 350°F and line a baking sheet with parchment paper.
2. Grab a large bowl and add the flour, cheese, cayenne and baking powder. Stir well.
3. Take another small bowl and whisk the egg. Throw this into the dry ingredients and mix well together. Add the cream and mix again.
4. Using your hands, take small spoonfuls of the mixture and form patties, popping them onto your pre-prepared baking sheet.
5. Place into the oven for 15 minutes then remove and allow to cool.
6. Pop into storage containers then serve when needed.
7. On serving day, serve with the suggested toppings, and enjoy!

Chocolate & Peanut Butter Keto Bites

Wow! Chocolate peanut treats! I know...I'm as excited as you are. But be aware that these do contain carbs (via the peanuts). Either omit them, replace with pili nuts or trim back your carbs from the rest of the day. Oh, and one final word, make more. They're soo good!

Serves: 4

Time: 25 mins

- Calories: 88
- Net carbs: 1.1g
- Protein: 1.7g
- Fat: 8.7g

Ingredients:

- 2 Tbsp. coconut oil
- 3 oz. peanut butter
- Drop vanilla extract
- 2 ½ tsp. cocoa powder
- 4 oz. ground almonds
- ½ tsp. sweetener
- 2 ½ tsp. chia seeds
- 1 ¾ Tbsp. coconut flakes, unsweetened

Method:

1. Grease a baking tray and pop to one side.
2. Take a bowl and add the peanut butter, cacao, sweetener, vanilla and coconut oil. Mix well.
3. Add the chia seeds and almond flour. Mix well.
4. Pile everything into your pre-prepared baking tray and press down.
5. Place into the freezer for 20 minutes until solid.
6. Cut into chunks and store in the freezer until needed.

Keto Marinara Sauce

Looking for a great marinara sauce which sticks to the Keto guidelines? Then try this one. The flavors work incredibly well together and there's no need for any nasty added sugar or preservatives.

Makes: 4 cups (nutrition per half cup)

Time: 5 mins

- Calories: 84g
- Net carbs: 3g
- Protein: 1g
- Fat: 7g

Ingredients:

- 28 oz. can peeled tomatoes
- ¼ tsp. black pepper
- ½ tsp. red pepper flakes
- 1 tsp. onion powder
- 1 tsp. garlic powder
- 1 tsp. dried basil
- 1 tsp. dried oregano
- 1 tsp. dried parsley
- 1 tsp. salt
- 1 Tbsp. red wine vinegar
- ¼ cup olive oil

Method:

- Place all the ingredients into your blender and hit that whizz button.
- Whizz until smooth.
- Store in the fridge until needed.

Worcestershire Sauce

Worcestershire sauce is a condiment which is practically IMPOSSIBLE to find without added sugar. So, let's make our own. Let's make it sugar-free, chemical-free and full of all that great taste you know and love.

Serves: lots of people! (nutrition per 1 tablespoon)

Time: 15 mins

- Calories: 8
- Net carbs: 1.73g
- Protein: 0.23g
- Fat: 0.07g

Ingredients:

- ½ cup beef stock
- 3 Tbsp. tomato paste, no salt and sugar added
- 1 Tbsp. aged balsamic vinegar
- 2 Tbsp. coconut aminos
- ¼ tsp. granulated onion powder
- ¼ tsp. garlic powder
- ¼ tsp. granulated mustard powder
- 1/8 tsp. sea salt
- 1/8 tsp. cinnamon powder
- 1/8 tsp. black pepper

Method:

1. Place all ingredients into a blender and hit whizz.
2. Pour into a medium pan, place over a medium heat and allow to simmer until the sauce thickens.
3. Remove from the heat, allow to cool completely, then pour into storage containers until needed.

Final words

If you want to watch the weight simply fall off whilst continuing to eat your favorite, tasty, appetite-satisfying, nutritious foods, the Keto diet is for you.

And if you want to save time and hassle in the kitchen, meal prep is definitely the life hack you need to master now.

Together, you have a rock-solid blueprint for health, wellness and a more productive life!

So don't just read this book, think *'Oooh, that's interesting'* and then just forget all about what you've read when the novelty has worn off.

Make it part of your life.

Commit to meal prepping at least one of your meals every day, whether that's breakfast, lunch, dinner or your snacks. Find what works, make this meal pre and Keto life *yours* and use the recipes I've included in this book to create amazing food time and time again.

Remember, don't think you have to pre-plan every morsel of food that crosses your lips in order to be a 'real' meal prepper. It doesn't work like that. Start small, do what you can, and the rest will follow.

Before I go...

I just want to say a big thank you for downloading this book. I hope you have enjoyed what you've read and will use the recipes I've gathered together to simplify your life, overhaul your health and shift that stubborn weight. If so, please take a second to leave me a quick review on Amazon. It all helps!

Nov 20 2021 204.4

Made in the USA
Middletown, DE
11 November 2018